KIAN SANCHEZ

Radiant Rebels

A Queer Guide to Unleashing Your Inner Fabulous

Contents

1

Embrace Your Rainbow Warrior Spirit

Setting the Stage

From ancient cave paintings to national flags, symbols throughout history have united communities, given voice to shared ideals, and stirred emotions that words alone cannot capture. Few emblems in modern times evoke such immediate resonance as the rainbow flag that has become the worldwide symbol of lesbian, gay, bisexual, transgender, and queer (LGBTQ+) pride and diversity.

The sight of those vibrant stripes undulating in the wind elicits an involuntary swell of emotion within many who have yearned for social acceptance or struggled against discrimination due to their sexual orientation or gender identity. The rainbow flag promises belonging, advocates liberation, and conveys an enduring sense of hope that the full spectrum of human diversity will one day be embraced.

The Birth of a Symbol

Symbols carry power.

To understand the potency behind such a seemingly simple vexillological design, we must appreciate the flag's emergence during a time of fear and uncertainty within the LGBTQ+ community. We must recognize how its colors and symbolism spoke directly to queer people's aspirations during the gay liberation movement. And we must witness how in just a few decades, this flag created by a little-known artist in San Francisco grew to become an internationally adopted emblem brandished proudly by millions each year during LGBTQ+ Pride Month celebrations around the globe.

The rainbow flag's origins echo those of the LGBTQ+ rights movement itself, grassroots in nature with a message that ignited hearts and minds much faster than its creator could have ever dreamed. The story begins in 1978 with Gilbert Baker, an openly gay activist and drag queen turned banner-maker, who saw the need for a new symbol under which the diversity of the queer community could find common cause.

While the pink triangle emblem had been reclaimed as a symbol of gay pride, its legacy bore the stain of Nazi persecution, forcing homosexual concentration camp prisoners to wear badges branded with upward-pointing pink triangles. Likewise, the Greek letter lambda had been adopted by some gay rights groups, inspired by the physics equation regarding wavelength with a metaphorical resonance aligning to the concept of light emerging from darkness. But Baker aimed higher, envisioning not just an icon but a banner behind which the kaleidoscopic LGBTQ+ community could march together with hope and harmony from self-loathing to self-love.

The rainbow was selected for its age-old symbolism spanning different eras and cultures, from biblical tales to optical science, almost universally conveying a bridge from stormy strife to bright renewal. This was the ideal metaphor for the burgeoning gay liberation movement in 1970s America seeking to rise above persecuted pasts through pride and visibility. By giving the rainbow shape and color in cloth, the symbol could now carry forth movement in a way no static graphic could ever convey.

Baker brought others into his home to help hand-dye and hand-stitch the first two rainbow flags in time for San Francisco's 1978 Gay Freedom Day Parade. What was first hoisted that June morning contained two additional colors alongside today's six-stripe standard— hot pink representing sex, and turquoise representing magic, nature, and art. Eyewitness accounts tell of tears instantly welling in marchers' eyes at the sight of their own vibrant banner proclaiming possibility and dignity blanketing the sky at last.

Yet the rainbow flag's adoption and resonance grew far more swiftly than its maker or admirers could have predicted. Despite Baker's intentions that the rainbow flag only be mass-produced through a nonprofit network granting proceeds back to social causes, entrepreneurial San Francisco shops immediately responded to public demand, commercially propagating the symbol on flags, T-shirts, pins, stickers and more. In this grassroots way through real people's pride and yearning for representation, the rainbow flag stepped beyond Baker's ideals and took on a life and legend of its own.

The years that followed bore witness to heartening and harrowing times as LGBTQ+ visibility and sociopolitical power rallied but also faced grave threats. And through it all, every community milestone, protest, vigil, celebration and riot shone under the brilliance of those striped rays of hope. The rainbow flag became the banner not only of lesbian and gayidentified movements but also for bisexual, transgender and more marginalized queer communities to rally under as they fought their own battles for recognition and equality over subsequent decades.

Today that original eight-color brilliance has been distilled to six, aligning symbolically to key aspects of queer diversity. Red represents life itself, orange evokes healing, yellow carries sunlight, green connotes nature's harmony, blue exalts artistry and magic, and violet honors the human spirit. These colors remain threaded together as one galvanizing spectrum, empowering modern allyship across the entirety of LGBTQ+ identities.

In the following chapters we will reflect on examples of the rainbow flag in action through recent history, gaining wider dimension on all this symbol has empowered and inspired. We'll trace provocative developments in its visibility within public arenas, from milestones in civic displays and commercial usage to backlash and even legislative attacks seeking to blunt this vibrant symbol's visibility and validity. We'll gain perspective on the myriad ways LGBTQ+ people and their allies continue innovating use of the rainbow flag to promote allyship and inclusion for communities and identities still marginalized under a mainstream concept of the emblem and movement it represents. And we'll envision how this iconic yet ever-evolving symbology shall continue to advance equality and dignity for all.

For now, as you first behold this spectrum rippling in wind or stillness, recognize the resonance it carries. Across distances, identities, languages and generations, the rainbow flag conveys struggle and celebration all at once, identity and openness to all. Its colors flow together in unity yet shine forth in individual brilliance, boldly flying in the face of all who would deny people's right to love and live freely. Waves of hope, waves of change…this is the power symbolized by a rainbow.

Decoding the Colors

A rainbow dazzles the eyes with its sweeping arc of spectral splendor. But when Gilbert Baker set out to gift the LGBTQ+ community with an emblem of unity and hope in 1978, he transformed the rainbow from atmospheric beauty into graphic power by giving each hue along its continuum a symbolic meaning all its own.

Red Life

The color red anchors one end of the rainbow flag palette, encapsulating the pulse of life itself. This vibrant wavelength, humming at the lowest frequency on the visible color spectrum, has signaled vitality and vigor across cultures and eras. Ancient societies including Chinese, Egyptian, and Native American tribes all recognized red as conveying primal life energy.

So when the original eight-color rainbow pride flag was born, red took its natural place as the foundational color embodying the LGBTQ community's collective strength and survival. After centuries of being pathologized as aberrant or criminalized as deviant, queer people were proclaiming their right not just to safely exist but to freely thrive within society. By leading with crimson, the rainbow flag's symbolism made clear that despite the HIV/AIDS crisis threatening gay men's very mortality at that time, this movement centered on advocating and celebrating the vibrancy of LGBTQ+ lives without compromise.

"I knew instantly why Gilbert chose red as the color to start the rainbow. Our community was just beginning to find coherence, to build itself into something so strong and beautiful as a rainbow. But it began with this foundation of red—the lifeblood that flowed through all of us queers no matter where we were," shares Lopez R., a 62-year-old queer Latinx activist who recalls his young adulthood marching beneath those first rainbow flags in the San Francisco Pride parades of the late 1970s.

"Back then, I had just come out to my very Catholic family. I showed up in San Francisco with no money and no direction. The rainbow flag welcomed me by saying I deserved to be alive as much as anyone. In red it told me, 'Keep breathing and keep fighting no matter who says otherwise,'" Lopez relates, his voice wavering. "Today, I think of that red stripe and remember queer youth still struggling with acceptance at home or bullied at school, wondering if their lives are worth living. I want them to know that red stripe flies for them too—they have so much life and love to give this world."

Through the height of the 1980s AIDS pandemic that saw society turn a cold shoulder while thousands died, that red stripe of the rainbow flag became blood-soaked in heartbreak but also in renewed anger and militant resilience. Red hot rage and resolve to fight back against indifference fueled activist groups like ACT UP (AIDS Coalition to Unleash Power) as the LGBTQ+ community recognized that direct action and disruption of the status quo offered their only hope with so many losses mounting amid government inaction.

"I was just a kid hearing the adults talk about 'gay cancer' while men in my neighborhood wasted away. Until suddenly it wasn't just adults talking anymore," explains Abby K., a 36-year-old bisexual woman from New York. "I lost two uncles—both gay, both denied hospital beds at the end because of bigotry. At their funerals when I was maybe eight years old, I remember seeing this sea of hundreds of AIDS activists outside wearing red ribbons and waving red flags. I didn't understand everything but I knew the red meant my uncles were heroes and that I was going to be part of fighting back when I was old enough. Every Pride since coming out in college, I wear red for the ones we lost too soon and for the fury to fight on in their honor."

The color red courses through myriad Pride events' costuming and messaging even today, honoring a history many witnesses now living never experienced firsthand. Red ribbons and apparel nod back to the symbolic "waves of red rage and resilience" that railed against sociopolitical systems failing the LGBTQ+ community when they literally faced life-and-death stakes. Through victories won incrementally and losses suffered unnecessarily, red persists as the color celebrating queer lives while also acknowledging this community's scrappy determination to survive and demand better when society still falls short.

Orange Healing

Transitioning from the hot-blooded crimson beginnings, orange makes its meaningful appearance as the second stripe in the rainbow flag's symbolic spectrum of significance. This secondary color blazing bright as Flame's very hue carries multiple meanings that fuel LGBTQ people's connection with its symbolic messaging.

On a primal level, orange inspires vitality, stimulating the senses and psyche in ways that rejuvenate body and boost mood. In chromotherapy healing traditions from Ayurvedic medicine to Reiki spiritualism, orange conjures natural uplift akin to soaking in the brilliance of dawn's first light after a long cold night. Decor designers employ the color judiciously for this energetic invigoration—a little orange goes a long way in enlivening entire spaces with its glow.

In the rainbow flag, orange beams bold and warm after the solemnity red holds as the roots of queer identity, history, and memory. With its sunrise-inspired dimension of renewal, orange conveys healing on multiple levels—physiological, emotional, communal and more. For LGBTQ people who've spent portions of life feeling fragmented, closeted or even self-loathing due to internal or external homophobia, embracing the orange stripe allows reclaiming wholeness and authenticity like daybreak reclaims the sky.

Brady L., a 30-year-old transgender man, declares orange his favorite hue in the rainbow for the self-affirmation it empowered during his transition journey:

"After two decades feeling like my own body was some alien shell I was trapped inside of, finally taking steps to affirm my male gender identity felt like waking up to my real self for the first time—like, 'Oh wow, it's YOU! Where have you been hiding?'" Brady recalls. "Every dose of hormone therapy felt like sunrise filling my veins. And the more I physically changed, the more everyone else could see my spirit burning brighter too. I healed years of disconnection from my own existence. Now orange will always glow for me like the very color of transformation."

Beyond this dimension of individual healing and personal embodiment, the rainbow's orange stripe also conveys healing justice for marginalized communities reckoning with sociocultural traumas. Just as red symbolically honors the staggering loss wrought by the 1980s AIDS pandemic in LGBTQ circles, orange signifies light finally penetrating that traumatic darkness through breakthrough medical advances and increasingly compassionate mental healthcare. And as consciousness expands around less visible health disparities disproportionately affecting LGBTQ+ individuals ranging from addiction to depression, orange beams more brightly signaling coalition-building across diverse advocates calling for improved understanding and access so queer populations can also claim their right to whole-person wellness.

"In my youth, therapists treated gayness as something to be cured while doctors viewed transness as mental illness outright. Health experts gave us no help, only more harm," laments Micah J., a 70-year-old non-binary pioneer who risked illegal gender-affirming medical transition to live authentically back in the 1960s. "The rainbow's orange stripe reconnects me to fellow survivors of that era's brutal discrimination masquerading as healthcare. But it also kindles hope that things keep getting better for trans youth accessing compassionate, affirmative treatment I never dreamed imaginable in my lifetime."

Inherently, something about orange pulls one's gaze upward and lifts the corners of the mouth, defying gravity's and grief's grim drag. Perhaps Emily Dickinson said it best in her poetic line extolling how "the color orange is like the sound of a horn." Within the rainbow flag, orange visually trumpets rejuvenation resonating back across miles, years, identities and generations of LGBTQ+ people ready to celebrate embodied authenticity without apology.

Yellow Sunlight

With orange already invoking daybreak's radiant return, it's only natural the spectrum soon shifts to yellow, compounding the solar symbolism as rainbow flag's third stripe. Since ancient times, cultures worldwide exalted yellow as capturing the very glow of our solar energy source, which all life relies upon. Across spiritual traditions from Egyptian iconography to Hindu lore, golden robes and visages anthropomorphized the sun and its capacity for imparting light and life, vision and vigor. Forward to medieval medicinal texts listing yellow's uplifting vibrations as panaceas for all manner of depression and melancholy. Fast forward again into 20th century metaphysics, where thinkers like Kandinsky theorized yellow conjures uniquely joyous emotion within human visual cortexes.

Indeed, cheerful connotations have trailed yellow through various eras and societies—sadness seems least sustainable in yellow's glow. Thus in the rainbow flag, sunny yellow carries layered meaning around illuminating previously shadowed or obscured corners of queer consciousness and community. In aspect it implores out-and-proud visibility after generations of LGBTQ existence and relationships hiding fearfully behind closed doors, drawn window shades, even darkened corners of public parks at peril of police raids after nightfall. Sharing the daylight together under yellow's guise became a radical act signaling refusal to accept stigma-induced isolation and second-class citizenship due to lovers or gender presentations deemed "other" by heteronormative convention.

"When I came out to my Puerto Rican family back in the 1990s, it felt scarier than staring into the sun since I couldn't predict if their reaction might burn me," admits Luz D., a 44-year-old lesbian. "But that year seeing activists marching together under a huge rainbow flag at Pridemade me feel bathed in righteous light, like this is who I'm meant to be in the open alongside my real family—chosen and self-made," she continues. "Every June going forward, I wore yellow remembering how unexpectedly bright life became living authentically without shadows even once my blood relatives disowned me."

Additionally, as historically LGBTQ+ individuals and relationships went overlooked or under documente in broader culture, social sciences, even family ancestries, yellow invites historically centered queer narratives to colorize these missing narratives, honor untold legacies that further humanize the full breadth of experiences shaping society. Ziggy P., now 63 years old and living proudly non-binary, reflects that:

"Back in grade school history lessons when stonewall inn raid or 'don't ask don't tell' controversies might have offered natural tie-ins to acknowledge queer people's presence and plight over time, such inclusion simply never occurred. The overall societal invisibility that erased our humanity got internalized within burgeoning young queer psyches in insidious ways difficult to shake," Ziggy notes. "Today's youth may actually feel excessive visibility being commodified and politicized before they're prepared to hold such heavy personal burdens. But for my generation, seeing that yellow stripe wave as an adolescent could have changed everything, emptying shadows we inhabited for decades."

By putting multi-hued LGBTQ+ narratives center stage in media and culture, by shining light into historical blindspots that long overlooked queer luminaries or minimized same-gender love stories mislabeled as mere friendship, by celebrating moments and movements advancing equality in public record and memory, yellow invites ongoing updates to dominant narratives that validate and enliven colorful queer existence as a treasured thread in humanity's shared tapestry.

Green Nature

Transitioning now toward the midpoint mark within the rainbow's symbolic spectrum, green makes its verdant visual proclamation as the next color charged with layered queer meaning. As the prevalent hue illuminating plant life across Earth's landscapes, green inherently connects to all things bodily and natural in popular consciousness. Human eyes even perceive green most vividly thanks to evolution equipping early hunter-gatherers to readily spot edible foliage on the move. So in the rainbow flag as in wider culture, green conveys compatibility with the natural realm rather than contention with or perversion of it as traditionally hetero-dominated society long accused anything LGBTQ+.

Brooklyn-based botanist and non-binary author Wren B. expounds: "Every phase of queer history echoes ongoing struggles to claim naturalness in who we love and how we self-identify," they explain. "The scientific racism used to denounce homosexuality as an aberrant mental illness was harder to uphold as more diverse human norms surfaced in wider study of global indigenous cultures. But trans and intersex bodily experiences remain pathologized as disordered... as if only two rigid biological sex presentations with no variance can constitute what's 'natural' for the human species!"

Wren continues describing how green's presence in the rainbow flag thus powerfully refutes such reductive binaries: "Through green the rainbow declares the full natural diversity of queer existence thriving bold and beautiful as any rainforest, ocean reef, bouquet of flowers or pride of lions!" Here Wren describes a symbolic invitation to move from fearing bodily or identity "otherness" within society toward celebrating shared participation in Earth's mosaic of nature unlimited by human hierarchies.

On a spiritual dimension, green also channels meaningful global mythos and increased modern meanings around unity, growth and harmony with nature for LGBTQ+ individuals. healers across indigenous shamanic traditions clad themselves in green to channel Earth energy and guide wounded souls back toward holistic wellness. Buddhism's green Tara remains revered across multiple Asian cultures as goddess of healing. Ancient Egyptian hieroglyphs prophesied that society's enlightenment equates to a "greening" of thought beyond fear-based tunnel vision that judges fellow humans' gender or sexual identities as right or wrong, real or fake, worthy or worthless according to limited lenses.

"When that sea of rainbow flags first waved over me as a baby dyke newly landed in San Francisco, I swear the green quieted my nerves most memorably," confides Sage I., now 49. "I grew up camping in Oregon's forests, always most at peace surrounded by nature. But I didn't foresee finding my people embracing me naturally too, allowing me to grow into myself under green's calming canopy of belonging."

Ultimately green invites embodying one's authentic nature without apology or camouflage, thriving as the individuals we were created to become. LGBTQ+ people inheriting a rainbow flag here find not only acceptance from fellow humans but also permission to root down more freely into one's divine soil, meditating into awakened states that reveal higher harmony regardless of how society's winds may bend or buffet. Exhaling fully into the vibrant green quadrant allows channeling perhaps that greatest invocation worth remembering: we are each other's ecosystem. And together, wondrous nature herself paints our flag's grand gesture skyward—naturally, without question or condition.

Blue Serenity

As the rainbow flag's color progression flows from nature's harmony into cooler tides midway along the spectral sequence, blue makes a soothing splash—in chromatic terms, tranquilly complementing the hot yellow-green vibrancy thus far. In cultures worldwide dating back through recorded history, blue pigment and lore conveyed equilibrium of mind and calm of mood. Crafters of heraldry, military uniforms, even nationwide insignia strategically utilize blue when imparting ideas around order, authority, collective focus.

Yet rarely does culture examine why blue elicits this stabilizing sentimental sway in human psyches. Scientific analysis reveals humans perceive blue most crisply of any color thanks to our eyes' retinas containing specialized "blue cones" solely dedicated to tuning into this specific light wavelength. Additionally these blue-tuned retinal receptors connect anatomically to brain circuitry controlling respiratory functions. So according to top neurologists' assessments, gazing at blue universally triggers physiological response that subconsciously regulates heartbeat, slows breath and thereby promotes calming chemical cascades throughout the nervous system.

Understanding these psychosensory mechanisms helps explain why the rainbow flag's blue stripe carries such centering potency amid the spectrum's rising emotional dynamics portrayed thus far. Having flowed from emboldening red life force through orange's invigorating dawn, yellow's illuminating emergence, and green's stabilizing authenticity, the blue wash introduces more meditative vibration. Here quilters like the late Gilbert Baker himself likened blue's effect to the traditional role sashing plays in patchwork design—frames each patch to enhance distinct beauty, emphasizes interconnectedness and unity in the greater pattern. For LGBTQ+ people rallying for solidarity under their rainbow, blue refocuses the collective gaze inward to recognize shared humanity beyond externally imposed labels.

"As a young runaway crashing on scary city streets after my parents kicked me out for being a sissy boy at 15, I felt shattered—dirty homeless scum according to most who saw me panhandling," admits Andre B., now 54. "But I would pick up discarded gay newspapers and hide out staring at ads for youth groups, health clinics, queer-friendly something," he continues. "That rainbow communicating in secret code only folks like me understood kept me sane… the blue told me silently 'just breathe, just rest.' I knew I wasn't alone even when it felt like no one cared if I lived or died."

Through such bleakest moments of internal turmoil or external endangerment aiming to tear down LGBTQ+ individuals' sense of peace or belonging, the rainbow's blue striping channels sturdy, forgiving foundations of self-regard. It conveys assurance that no outside instability sabotages inherent inner calm rooted in self-knowing one's equal right to inhabit this planet without justification and exist exactly as spirit created. For many modern queer people assured safer protections and freedoms than previous generations, blue takes on further applied meaning around transmitting tranquil ripples into society's remaining margins where turmoil still rages through hateful policies or extreme homophobia denying LGBTQ+ humanity still.

Leanne P. a 48-year-old lesbian describes: "Too many pride events now feel more centered on corporate float sponsorships than communicating care and empowerment for the ongoing crises disproportionately killing trans women of color, displacing queer homeless youth, allowing suicide and violence thrive where religion demonizes LGBTQ+ souls," she notes. "I still proudly wave that rainbow for all it represents, but I make a point focusing blue wavelength energy first while singing chants to send loving kindness to the periphery so everyone feels safe to come in and heal."

Purple Spirit

Crossing now into the rainbow spectrum's final frequencies reveals cooler hues brewing rich purpose. Where red began our symbolic sequence Pulsing hot with the tangible realities of queer culture and community shouldered over generations, the journey culminates awash in purple posing far more abstract and philosophical turns of thought.

Western religions drape priests and royals in violet to convey sacred wisdom and status nearest the divine. Both cultural perspectives clearly revere the potency purple symbolizes illuminating the intricate eternal essence inhabiting these mere mortal vessels over time.

So when the rainbow flag immersed 1970s LGBTQ communities in a unifying vibration of validity and liberation after eons awaiting light, what color could more fittingly crown the burgeoning movement's clarion banner but transcendent violet? Choosing purple as the noble crest communicating highest vibration, the rainbow flag's original crafters summoned ancient hereditary meaning around supreme wisdom, sovereignty of self, sacred covenant beyond society's constraints.

Violet here exalted queer folks from persecuted pariahs through to rightful royals crowned by their own self-determined identities and self-love supreme. Too long had LGBTQ lives lost meaning condemned under laws and overlords measuring existence by narrow heteronormative standards. Now in violent's rich beauty glimmering atop their jubilant new flag, a banner of belonging embraced identities and relationships outside rigid social scripts as equally divine expressions love bestowed without hierarchy.

"I instantly bawled when I caught first glimpse of that homemade rainbow flag draped proud outside a SF commune, maybe 1977?" recalls 81-year-old Trevor S. among pioneering activists present at the rainbow symbol's birth. "Young people today call me dramatic, but you must understand my generation endured police literally raiding our parties, seizing guests, beating many to death purely for living free and gay back when the whole world called that a disorder, perversion or crime," Trevor emphasizes, voice still pained yet proud from across the decades. "So can you imagine suddenly seeing OUR COLOR, violet majesty blanketing this brand new flag above our streets? That, my dears, was heaven declaring WE mattered finally too! After all history said otherwise!"

Indeed the pall purple cast always evoked queer resonance—century-old poems coined "the love that dare not speak its name" in reference to coded homosexual affairs. Ancient Mediterranean royals clad boy lovers in violet robes signifying such trysts conducted under noble auspices immune from common condemnation. Back through artists DaVinci to Prince projecting implicitly queer personas in modern eras but purpling their images whether flaunting Renaissance blouses or 1980s ruffled glam, violet visuals grew steeped in subtle signalling to LGBTQ+ eyes awakening through the ages.

So when that rainbow flag debuted in 1978 literally stitching violet liberation skyward as its pinnacle stripe in San Francisco just one year post-Anita Bryant's national "Save Our Children" anti-gay crusade, such prominence proclaimed no more hiding in humiliation. This bright yet complex purple at the rainbow's edge reflected dawning realization within queer communities: only embracing out full divine individuality could usher society from demonizing difference toward upholding dignity equally, understanding love's, gender's kaleidoscopic breadth as spiritual riches not threats warranting attacks.

"I was an exiled Mormon kid on Utah's streets escaping electroshock therapy church & family forced to 'fix my affliction,'" 29-year-old trans writer Jory K. relates. "Stealing an LGBT newspaper introduced me not only to resources that changed my life but also that rainbow flagcover declaring some unseen upside-down world where purple means you BELONG for living out and proud," Jory continues. "That purple stripe still inspires my banner today encouraging fellow questioning Mormon kids too scared to come out back home: just embrace your beautiful true violet spirit waiting to rise when the timing is right!"

Even when the rainbow flag temporarily tapered its spectrum from original eight colors down to six for visibility's sake as it mobilized in wider rallies through the late '70s/early '80s, violet pointedly persisted as the pinnacle color crown. And in recent decades as intersectional queer activism matured to uplift LGBTQ voices of color, differently abled queers, two-spirit indigenous teachings and more, violet's significance only expands as the rainbow's highest shade promoting radical self-regard for peoples historically robbed of any self-love foundation by colonial forces.

Ace A., a formerly homeless 18-year-old transgender Arapaho two-spirit youth, describes reconnecting to their indigenous identity through modern embodiments of the rainbow flag's symbolic messaging: "After my family rejected me, only seeing that purple waving every June reminded me I couldn't be that wrong or sinful if Creation blessed some people like me with special gifts and medicine to share by bridging masculine/feminine spirit realms others access one-dimensionally," they relate. "But discovering updated Pride flags like Philadelphia's black/brown added stripes honoring queer/trans POC communities helped me recognize the rainbow can exclude voices like Two Spirit teachings. So now I hand-bead my own purple feathers onto rainbow patches and bracelets to stay rooted in my ancestors' traditions while celebrating myself."

Ultimately, the rainbow flag's violet stripe continues evolving as a symbol reminding LGBTQ people to look beyond limiting human words or white-dominant cultural worldviews that historically demonized queer identities…and instead read one's worth through a lens of divine self-love. In white-centric, cishet-dominated Western societies, cisgender heterosexuality centered as the societal "default" which all else deviates from. Generations of queer youth internalized the implicit messaging that falling outside such norms made one fundamentally wrong, unworthy, even condemned—a belief often reinforced by cultural institutions like church theology and psychiatric diagnostic labeling that further instilled internalized shame and self-loathing. Stars including Lil Nas X and JoJo Siwa describe only recently overcoming such heavily internalized self-judgement after decades spent battling their own treasured talents and truths judged as too flamboyantly gay for mass acceptance.

Yet the subtly coded salvation symbolized through violet always awaited resonating and liberating LGBTQ hearts who found solace in things grouping just beyond cis-hetero paradigms. Visionaries from Sappho to Sylvia Rivera shone brightest activating creative gifts lifted from suffering the margins where rigid social systems couldn't comprehend the precious way wisdom blooms when we express ourselves freely. So as queer thinkers and truth-tellers carry on this ethical legacy in modern eras, rallying for not only LGBTQ dignity but all humanity's growth toward more radically inclusive justice, the rainbow's violet stripe continues flying highest for what even leading minds and faiths don't yet grasp but unapologetic violet spirits just intrinsically understand through and through.

Embracing the Warrior Spirit

The rainbow flag undulates proudly as an international symbol of LGBTQ+ identity, unity and advocacy. Yet notably absent from most vexillology discourse and rainbow iconography is acknowledgement of what fuels such vibrancy channeling at times against violently oppressive political winds.

Behind the rainbow's brilliance beats a pulse of courageous resilience, which we might term the Rainbow Warrior Spirit. This references the long lineage of scrappy nonviolent "warriors" who sacrificed greatly fighting for civil rights and social justice reforms. But it also names a mindset or sense of purpose emboldening LGBTQ+ people and allies to stand firm in their truth and advance equality amid adversity.

Cultivating one's own Rainbow Warrior Spirit proves essential for queer individuals seeking to live openly and authentically in environments less than accepting, though its bold framework for self-actualization serves all who wrestle internal shadows or external barriers hindering self-love and purposeful advancement. Revisiting lives of inspirational leaders who came before lights the way forward. We might recognize the Rainbow Warriors' legacy in early homophile organizations publishing newsletters daring to use the word "gay." Or in the transgender patrons at Stonewall Inn literally fighting back against police oppression with their high heels in a seminal 1969 stand for human rights.

But Rainbow Warriors walk among us to this day, still overcoming overt discrimination or subtle discouragement aiming to dim their light. Hearing their stories not only uplifts from wishful thinking into expanded possibility for one's own path ahead. It also clarifies the meaning of pride for those who honor such legacies by celebrating visibility and progress yet acknowledging the distance left to go before LGBTQ+ people enjoy equal access, safety and dignity worldwide.

Surviving to Thriving

Creighton T. exudes Rainbow Warrior Spirit simply entering a room. Their radiant non-binary presence enlivens any occasion through quick wit and wisdom earned surviving years homeless after family rejection. In high school Creative endured corrective rape and exorcism rituals aiming to "pray away the gay." Though they managed completing diploma studies homeless and addicted, two stints in prison followed.

"Yet my worst days still proved better than returning to that household telling me I was ungodly," they reflect. "I clawed toward freedom any way possible."

Lead with Love

verbose transphobia attempted blocking Alex Mar's trailblazing run for public office. Some rivals even outright threatened Alex's personal safety unless they dropped pursuit of Vermont's Congressional seat as an openly nonbinary candidate.

Biut Alex led first with love while standing firm in their resolve. "Hurt people hurt people,' they reminded their campaign. "Meet ignorance and fear with empathy…thenBallte it through education ant joy."

Their team echoed Alex's resilient messaging through policies uplifting both marginalized LGBTQ+ communities and economically struggling rural regions their opponents dismissed. And voters responded to Alex's promise: "Leading with listene first ears and open hearts pulls us all higher."

AlexMar made history as the first nonbinary candidate elected to U.Sr Congress. In their victory speech Alex characteristically credited supporters: "Rainbow Warrior Spirit shone in those who believed humanity brave enough to embrace progress together." They concluded reiterating their campaign's core motto progressing inclusive representation: "Wherever you are on your journey, lead with love…and love will lead the way."

Creative Resistance

Quantasia s. expresses her Rainbow Warrior brand of brilliance through pageantry platforms initially hosting her as their first transgender titleholder with grave ambivalence until Quantasia's gracious grit stunned spectators. Though initially permitted to enter under duress, event coordinators coached Quantasia to downplay her transness. "They expected I wouldn't have a chance if openly discussing medical transition specifics," Quantasia recalls.

Though privately hurt by such attempts to tone down her visibility and voice, Quantasia grew determined amplifying trans narratives would prove central to her participation. Her interview response to "Who in history inspires you" celebrated groundbreaking trans actor Laverne Cox and author Janet Mock for bolding advancing intersectional representation. Quantasia's costume for the talent segment proudly incorporated trans flag colors with body-positive messaging. Through the final gala Quantasia awarded her systems title sash to her mother who lovingly embraced Quantarsia's coming out despite extended family objections.

Judges initially scored Quantasia low for flouting expectations to assimilate. Yet audience support swelled for her authenticity until coordinators had no choice but to crown Quantarsia in acknowledgment of the people's choice. "Rainbow Warriors lead hearts and minds through creativity before might makes right," Quantarsia says of how she conducted her platform. Her example demonstrates grace under unjust pressure can shift perspective from regression into growth affirming out loud what many know fair in whispered solidarity.

As we witness such bold momentum within LGBTQ+ movements at the same time fringes dig in more desperately clinging to old biases packaged as "traditional values," may remembering what Rainbow Warrior Spirit survived through generations past reinforce soft power courage to advance justice today. Not rage but radical love lifts all. Not riot but creative truth-telling shifts consciousness. Therein lies reclaimed pride and armor against all that still threatens it.

Cultivating Rainbow Warrior Mindset

The term "warrior spirit" may conjure militaristic aggression incongruent with LGBTQ+ philosophies around nonviolence and returning harm with compassion. But Rainbow Warriors understand that strategic peaceful resistance demands its own form of courage and vigilant persistence upholding dignity, essence and shared humanity until oppressive mentalities relent.

Cultivating personal resilience through a Rainbow Warrior lens empowers countering unjust policies or interpersonal biases with centered confidence versus reactionary rage that can undermine moral messaging. Try these practices for fostering your own Warrior Spirit lifeline, allowing external negativity to roll past like water as you stand tall planted in your truth.

Connect to ancestry - Research lineages and locales your genetics hail from. Consider the radical ideas, struggles or conditions that shaped your inheritance. Feel the fighters' feisty pulse still flowing through your veins, their vindication living on through you.

Define your purpose - Warrior Spirit links to one's sense of purpose and principles providing strength. Outline what unique impact you hope your life imprints on the planet. What talents or experiences make you specially qualified to uplift which perspectives or needs in the world around you? Discover your quest.

Practice mindfulness - Injustice can breed reflexive bitterness if we let oppression's barbs pierce our open wounds. Train response versus reaction through mindful movement or meditation that lets negativity wash past like a river around stone. Breathe consciously to broaden perspective and sustain balanced action aligned to purpose.

Foster community - Even the bravest spiritual warriors relied on solidarity circles for counsel and courage-boosting. Identify which chosen family kinsfolk or mentorship links affirm your essence and expand your empowerment. Connect in person when possible but also digitally given geographic barriers.

Celebrate symbols - External icons from tattoos to jewelry build motivation through symbolic meaning you directly imbue. The veterans' Dog Tags brand and Pink Triangle reclaimed unite Pride and protest power. Display symbols signifying your identity and inspirations made tangible.

Give gratitude - Even on the darkest days or when stuck in stressful situations largely out of control, actively list 5 to 10 blessings fueling appreciation. This ritual neurologically overrides panic instincts, enhances resiliency against depression. Send silent gratitude to figures who paved the way for more rights and representation today.

Spread light - Warrior spirit stewards inner light outward to ignite wicks in other hearts till enough shine with shared truth that ignorance cannot hide from dawning realization. Uplift fellow humans who need kind counsel or advocacy through actions small and large.

Take inspired action - Beyond armchair activism, determine what bold frontline footwork only your distinct voice and vantage can accomplish to advance inclusive justice and hold ground retaken in earlier equality battles. Localize change through global movements uniting unlikely allies.

The quest for human rights and soulful liberation has never required uniformity, only solidarity around sacred visions for peace and possibility. By following the footsteps and blazing new trails illuminating through crimson, orange, green, purple prisms of tenacity tasted by those who came before, may we each find fitfully that warrior resilience ever rallying its radiance through onward, inward, upward, onward.

Unleash Their Warrior Within

What an extraordinary journey we have shared delving behind the brilliant colors and bold symbolism that imbue the LGBTQ+ rainbow flag with such power across eras and borders. In exploring the stories and spirit this banner has come to embody since first fluttering into San Francisco's winds just over 40 years ago, we more fully comprehend all that resonates in its rippling rays today.

We learned how one artist's humble vision for stitching together a unifying emblem of diversity quickly took on a life and legend of its own as LGBTQ+ people rallied beneath its colors for visibility, solidarity and celebration of identities no longer content living in the shadows. We gained perspective on the painful yet proudly defiant histories evoked in the flag's progressive stripe sequence...from the urgent crimsons of raw life or blood spilled too soon, through oranges kindling protective pride and sacred healing inside us that no outside attack can entirely extinguish.

Vibrant yellows invite stepping fully into sunlight's validation, while verdant greens ground us confidently upon Mother Earth's canvas blooming all of nature's uninhibited splendor. Across the spectrum, tranquil blues call forward calm perspective amid any surrounding storms before visionary violets crown every identity equally with sacred self-love inherited as divine birthright yet too often denied across societies slow to acknowledge LGBTQ+ humanity.

Thus through contrasts and blends of light defined via photons yet enlivened through you and me, the rainbow's nested imagery compels outstretched hands, upturned gaze and irrepressible hope.

This is why even those joyfully witnessing great leaps in LGBTQ+ equality and acceptance over recent generations continue flying the flag with reverent gratefulness for the painful roads behind that carried us to widening horizons at last promising safer harbors ahead. Understanding where we have been and how symbolically we keep those humbling lessons waving near steadies us for times when storms again darken or resistance to change distracts the collective eye from all who still yearn for compassion.

Perhaps you as reader drew open these pages out of casual curiosity, seeking insight around a prominent yet poorly understood cultural emblem suddenly surfacing more routinely in your experience. Or maybe you were lured by a longing to reconnect to your own winding odyssey toward self-love as an LGBTQ+ person or ally also instructed by this spectrum's light along portions of your authentic journey. Either way, may you complete this first glimpse upon our shared standard feeling more firmly rooted in its historic significance, resolved to lift it higher in guiding your growth and guardianship henceforth!

Recall how this living legacy was literally hand sewn to convene and hearten a community too long tattered by suffocating norms. But with nothing more than stranded threads of scrapped fabric and dye trailing holistic meaning across ages into cross-cultural consciousness, this humble banner both acknowledged injustice and beckoned unified response upholding our universal right to breathe, love and be through every brilliant color manifesting life's full positive, healing potential. May we honor such origins by refusing complacency with how far liberty has come compared to earlier decades of gospel shouting "no" against our very sense of being. Until "pride" equates defending dignity equally, not just celebrating some cities' glittering parades, we must honor the symbol by battling all erosions of progress through compassion wielding truth as sharp and dazzling as any double-edged sword.

This chapter's exploration of the global icon this movement made mainstream hardly captures comprehensive context or chronicles behind the rainbow emblem's meaning and might accelerating still today. Yet in imparting even such introductory impressions, may seeds of curiosity take root in your conscience so sufficiently to seek deeper roots reaching toward richer rainbow relevance!

The next chapters survey specific developments in this flag's prominence and purpose across eras and communities continuing to refine its rainbow resonance. From its sudden ubiquity blanketing popular media and commerce to purposeful appropriations adapting the rainbow motif to highlight still-marginalized LGBTQ+ demographics and dynamics, both the banner's broader messaging and very structure shifts across generations of queer activists answering earlier generations' calls for solidarity and change.

Wherever you find yourself on spectrums of identity or interest around rainbow flag lore, hoist high your own perceptions with willingness to question, clarify and grow them. Who remains yet excluded from the rainbow's promise in your surroundings that community efforts might consciously better envelope? Does mainstream privilege anywhere overshadow almost ironic isolation for those whose battles remain less won? How might you steward more colors, more courage toward inclusive justice where old nicely shifts into new narratives balancing and uplifting all?

Such self-inventory fuels the fighter within, that bold Rainbow Warrior Spirit ever on guard against complacency of belief that while laws and leniencies legitimize some, all queer people currently claim their birthright liberties equitably across earth. May you take up bespoke strands of the great banner's legacy through emboldened personal purpose only your distinctive essence can champion. Our shared humanity shall surge lifted thus upon this flag's tide and our hearts harmonize honed sharp against ignorance yet offered open through unconditional positive regard. And so with ink as light for pages now ending yet insight still dawning, we ready pens and pulses alike to write the rainbow's next victorious chapter in our times.

2

Queer Eye for Your True Self

The Power of Transformation

A subtle yet monumental shift ripples through popular culture as reality makeover shows like Queer Eye remodel both living spaces and perspectives. Beyond redecorating environments or revamping wardrobes, the show's premise presents personal transformation as an inside job—the work begins with radically re-envisioning how one relates to oneself.

Onscreen the Fab Five descend to modernize straight male subjects' aesthetic aptitude across home, grooming, fashion, cuisine and confidence domains. Yet the biggest reveals emerge less from surface-level ambiance adjustments and more from moving stories of internal metamorphosis sparked through compassionately candid mirrors this dream team holds up. As voices historically pushed to society's fringes, the Fab Five tap personal experiences contending with others' narrow perceptions to expand their subjects' self-limiting mindsets.

And with intricately interwoven emotional support plus skillful style guidance, the show charts profound identity shifts subtly paralleling physical makeovers. Subjects express feeling more aligned, alive and authentically seen. By welcoming contrasting perspectives, they move beyond internalized hangups that previously hindered self-expression. Through playful disruption of familiar spaces and routines ruptured open to welcome expanded possibility, transformation unfolds.

Yet one needn't await a famous lifestyle crew's arrival to reboot one's own self-image and environments reflecting back evolving truths within. The Venn diagram housing outer image and inner essence provides ample creative workspace for reviving self-love and purpose when we claim authority as the artist in charge. Just as a rainbow's colors shine unique prisms yet intermingle as one, so too can even modest experiments donning underutilized personal strengths or passions more boldly expand our self-concept integrating parts long fragmented in shadows.

The Psychology of Self-Expression

Decades before television offered today's immersive makeover entertainment, trailblazing psychologist Carl Jung identified identity evolution as the work of a lifetime. According to Jung, persona represents the version of self we present to society—the metaphoric masks we wear across varied interpersonal roles and settings over years, compromising certain demands to uphold distorted ideals of who we "should" become based on inherited biases. Yet under such necessary public pretenses that broker external validation, our sovereign soul-self remains longing for fuller expression and embrace of the most authentic inner realities challenging yet enriching once allowed enough air and light.

Jung labeled such unrealized elements of one's identity the "Shadow Self"—a concept suggesting not some sinister split personality but rather positive potency kept closeted when deemed too far outside acceptably narrow personality norms taught since childhood. Reintegrating denied fragments of self-hood allows transcending previously limiting scopes on who we permit ourselves to be and become in the world. But according to Jung it demands courageously wearing socially countercultural colors that often initially feel garishly loud, embarrassingly tight or alarmingly sheer when compared against familiar ego costumes molded by others' expectations over years spent assimilating.

Yet just as Meadow Williams or Bobby Berk might function as on-set spirit guides coaxing fearful Fab Five initiates toward more accurate self-expression through style, so too can we enlist intuitive parts already recognizing which accessories or hues best broadcast our inner rainbow. Experimenting playfully with these identity ingredients mixing and remixing liberates new directions. What once seemed jarringly "unprofessional" or "inappropriate" eventually feels wonderfully authentic with enough modeling and positive reinforcement. Soon the essence that always existed at our core flows freely through forms navigating the world visibly validated versus stifled chronically behind facades.

Pushing Boundaries Through Self-Expression

Permission to play and creativity incubate even small tweaks advancing alignment of values and appearance can unlock radical redefinition. Fashion provides one of the most common vehicles. Think combat boots believing themselves best suited for punk songs or poetry scribbled privately in notebooks before gaining courage donning editor's inboxes. Either way, looks manifest chosen values. Costumes keep company with consciousness itself.

"For years I wore nothing but beige and grey trying to disappear within corporate cubicles," recalls non-binary entrepreneur Alex T who recently launched an LGBT-owned street wear line after initially perceiving such vibrant self-expression as off-limits given past career constraints.

"I had so much creative energy and leadership ability that I couldn't channel stuffed in those suits. Getting laid off is what catapulted my coming out journey and taking the risk of funding my own company celebrating identities beyond binaries. Now I'm out and proud in crop tops, jumpsuits, feathers and sequins like I always dreamed. My company's values literally wear people now as apparel affirming free gender expression that my old bosses would have deemed 'unprofessional.' Turns out that radical authenticity was my most powerful professional asset just waiting in the wings."

Alex's example demonstrates Jung's emphasis on embracing the Shadow Self not as means of demolishing productive aspects of the persona altogether but rather broadening its flexibility to include wider bandwidths of our sovereign nature. Indeed across industries, psychological research links even peripheral self-expression tweaks with cognitive advantages from enhanced original thinking to improved task focus and retention. quantifiable workplace perks like increased productivity and workplace morale further incentivize corporate cultures to relax outdated conservative grooming codes and dress policies now proven reductionist. Mental health fields similarly shifted away from pathologizing identities and presentations straying beyond majority concepts of gender or orientation normalcy as inherently disordered.

Outside such formal environments, interpersonal exchanges invite more default acceptance these days around pronouns, partners and passions signaled across ever-expanding identity lexicons. Still, bias and discrimination persist in ways subtle and overt wherever minorities assert self-concepts contravening traditional mainstreams. No doubt additional tensions (and teachable moments) shall continue flaring as social consciousness collision courses correct and overcorrect. But the quest toward equitable liberty and justice for all gender identities and sexual orientations presses forward fueled by the fiery fruits of full authentic expression at last lighting torches for some who walk paths still craving cultural validation.

Setting the Stage for Transformation

So in spacious spirit of resisting either/or extremes as societal tensions tussle, consider overriding internalized inhibitors by honoring nuance. Allow your identity's disparate aspects dialogue decoding the external environments and inner ecosystems best supporting your growth across passing seasons. Which version of self warrants welcoming from shadows this month, this year, this lifetime? What parts of your being benefit from spotlighting a while atop center stage in some scene or chapter presently unfolding?

Rather than reacting fearfully toward identities contrasting one's own, radical self-expression invites leaning curiously into exponential abundance unlocked when peoples overlay, underplay or own previously disowned colors of their complex personhood with boldness scrawling self-definitions impossible to mistake as anything other than beautifully bespoke. What dormant dreams or dimensions of your kaleidoscopic character contain necessary notes in the human song yearning through you for voice this day? Might you harmonize more loudly, beautifully or on beat by bypassing filters forged in past external fires but no longer serving the primal music within?

Likely no television crew can congeal customized catalysts clarifying such innermost growth paths for you as astutely as your own intuitive rumination. But through these pages we comb interconnected insights from contemporary culture and depth psychology into digestible tools anyone can access appraising identity aspects seeking amplification or adjustment to write forthcoming chapters resonating true. By playfully surveying our own terrain more wholly exactly as we are in each given moment, external upgrades unlocked across inner landscapes harvest happiness letting our essence shine colorized, dimensional and unapologetically dynamic at last.

Personal Stories of Transformation

While dramatic makeovers might make for compelling viewing on screens, everyday life writes the real legends through quiet revolutions kindling one courageous choice at a time. Across the intricate spectra of human experience, glimpses into others' journeys can inspire our own next steps toward transformation through radically aligned self-expression.

Unlearning Shame, Relearning Style

"I grew up heir to hand-me-downs, relying on thrift store rubble to clothe me through childhood poverty and my teens equally impoverished of self-worth thanks to peers tormenting me for dull donated threads," recalls writer Willa J. of coming of age closeted across both gender and economic margins in the early 2000s. "I internalized those bullies and messages mandating in order to earn respect or intimacy, I must upgrade my entire existence."

Willa describes relentlessly chasing conventional beauty standards through cosmetic procedures, designer knockoffs and excessive overspending aiming to mask perpetual unbelonging – until catastrophe corrected course. "Losing almost everything in a house fire, I suddenly gained perspective. None of the logos, lip fillers or loot fulfilled me anyway because I never bothered bonding with the spirit inside longing to embrace quirky sensibilities society shamed."

In ashes of lost possessions, glamour's illusion lifted allowing Willa to reconsider outdated assumptions that muted personal style signaled meager character. Over subsequent years speaking vulnerably through published memoirs then rallying public outreach countering capitalists' churn and burn messaging, Willa's authenticity won adoration no glossy disguise ever could.

"Funny how in losing the external stamp of approval through fame or 'luxury' status I gained meaningful connection and community that actually validated me for me. Now I celebrate identity daily through bold prints, wild textures and experimental shapes emboldening lifelines society tries severing when we dare live loudly."

Health Over Hiding

Caleb N. endured decades camouflaging his HIV positive status in professional spheres leery of queer sexuality and illness' supposed limits. He masked chronic health struggles under workaholic tendencies weathering long hours, skipped self-care and silently suffering side effects strained workplaces proved ill-equipped accommodating.

Over years Caleb watched identity and immune function atrophy in equal proportions plummeting productivity further. Rare lunch breaks he spent alone while colleagues bonded, his silence and weight loss apparent yet breaching taboos around discussing disease or diversity difficulties in corporate climates. HR offered little help; Caleb couldn't afford losing insurance coverage if terminated.

Yet fate forced transparency when one opportunistic infection landed Caleb hospitalized at death's door. Surprisingly survivor support flooded forthcoming once fanatically career-focused coworkers. "Ironically job performance review boards cut me more slack than I gave myself trying to hide HIV battle," Caleb admits. "Now weekly work forums address eliminating assumptions around invisible disabilities or POW medical journeys."

Caleb co-founded workplace wellness initiatives securing healthcare extensions and flexible arrangements allowing him to refuel through self-care and purpose beyond profit margins. "Funny how fully expressing personal health truths publicly ended up humanizing professional spaces for multitudes," he notes. "My own locked shadows found keys to free suppressed voices and policies aiding more to walk proudly in our power."

Journey Over Destination

Allison R.grasped at goalposts for years chasing external reflections of achievement but found fleeting solace. She hustled straight As steering toward moneyed careers seeking parental pride, plowed through Ivy League yet felt increasingly empty. In marathon drives to make partner by thirty she forfeited bonding with partners or social lives outside work.

"No business class stamp of approval filled voids inside after burning out completely en route corporate fortune without deeper purpose," Allison admits. "I lived too long letting strangers define metrics for meaning and happiness before recognizing only I own wisdom what shapes significance my life's dash between dates."

During recovery connecting causes kindling personal passion not societal pedigree, Allison found purpose mentoring diverse youth exploring careers breaching usual gender roles. Volunteering weekends at animal shelters and queer nonprofit boards surfaced satisfying rhythms community contributed missing more than solitary success climbing ladders now seeming leaned against wrong walls.

Allison resigned lofty law firm posts to launch an LGBTQ+ owned bakery whose sweet sales fund expanded counseling for foster kids aging out of systems. "Now I proudly claim this collared shirt with rainbow flag and 'Founder' stitching as the only external label lending enough legitimacy to please me," she smiles. "Ironically in ditching dean's list I discovered distinctions that actually satisfy my soul."

The deepest transformations often whisper gradual metamorphosis through unassuming acts slowly yet wholly restructuring who we know ourselves to be like glaciers grinding granite. Yet sudden landslides also impact identity by forces beyond our control, urgently necessitating navigation skills too seldom taught. Either way the journey inward always pilots progress more than mere arrival could. In whatever chapters or scenes await around your bend, may looking within guide all without astray.

Identifying Your Authentic Style

Surveying stories of others' metamorphosis through aligned identity upstairs and down primes perspective for traversing your own self-expression topography more intentionally. By examining influences that imprinted certain sensory aesthetics over time, you gain agency editing the narrative's next chapter. Trailblazers demonstrate detouring beyond societal constraints or internalized messaging limiting how we occupy privileged roles as protagonists of our sovereign storyline.

But understanding origin stories underpinning current comfort zones helps rewrite limiting rules. Consider which personal politics, cultural customs or family traditions shaped ideas around acceptable apparel, textures, scents and other sensory stimulations in the habitat called "you." Then dare imaging those environs redesigned radically through rebellious redecoration affirming authentic essence over assimilating.

Understanding Your Style Story

To author the next chapter aligned to inner truth, first acknowledge key characters and plot points forming your style saga thus far. Contemplate questions like:

What aesthetics did childhood surrounding culture celebrate most? Which seemed subtly sanctioned as off-limits and why?

Were frills and florals coded feminine against dominate machismo traditions? Did grandparents guardians ever decree certain fabrics too flashy, hemlines too short, volumes too loud or colors clashing according to their generation's standards?

Which influencers impressed values around self-presentation upon you most memorably?

Maybe maternal figures monitored every mirror's reflection scanning for perceived imperfections to fixate upon. Or perhaps peer social scenes policed admission through unspoken style protocols that keyed access by branding and trendiness. Consider whose messaging influenced self-judgment.

When did your own tastes first contradict inherited expectations around looks?

Puberty piercings hidden under mandated hair lengths—a singlet smuggled secretly under stuffy ceremonial wear. Tiny trials tested limits before bolder experiments like pixie cuts, tattoos or gender fluid fashion flowed forth. Highlight moments that widened bandwidth of expression.

Which current sociocultural spaces welcome wide creative self-expression most? Which still restrict?

While corporate climates grew more casual, certain career costumes still signal success across industries. Places of worship, ceremony and tradition often mandate conformity calibrating creative freedom. Even Instagram's highlight reels homogenize visible identities lobbying luxury. Map where you can relax most authentically.

Who most validated you for simply being yourself without styling alteration?

When did you feel seen and safe exploring identity facets beyond those family, faith or greater society deemed digestible? Which chosen family kindred spirits or intimate partners proved loyal applauding experiments outside customary boxes even when uncomfortable at first? These relationships reflect reserves affirming creative renewal.

How might revisiting past style eras channel healing?

Reconnecting favorite textures, asserting heirloom accents confidently despite outdatedness or even daring full aesthetic emulations of looks from earlier chapters spent assimilating grounds growth in good memories that shaped us prior periods of poor self-concept contorting natural preferences to conform.

Practicing Personal Style as Self-Care

Just as Fab Five grooming guru Jonathan Van Ness emphasizes self-care rituals that nurture neglected nervous systems beyond busy-ness, consider curating aesthetic environments and experiences specifically soothing parts too long overlooked or overworked.

Create a vision board collaging styles that compel: Gather inspiring images, fabric swatches, color palettes, clothing editorials etc. appreciating visual styles resonating allure. Display selections prominently for regular reflection.

Catalog current wardrobe contents assessing fits: Inventory which beloved pieces boost confidence versus items inciting doubts that now warrant donating. Curate capsule collection in empowering colors/textures/silhouettes evoking authenticity.

Schedule sensory-rich shopping inspiration sessions: Visit alternative boutiques without pressure purchasing; simply appreciate artistry. Museums and cultural festivals similarly stimulate sartorial senses.

Designate long weekends for playful exploration: Dress freely fusing facets typically compartmentalized professional versus personal. Blend eras with elements evoking past chapters now viewed through bold lens.

Claim finishing touches that uniquely you: Whether tattoos, scarves or statement glasses, accessorize joyfully. Adorning environments similarly calibrates energetic alignment—display heirlooms, plants, colors kindling calm.

Unplug perfectionist reflexes for fun: Improvise freely through movement or creative mediums without self-judgment. Playful flow channels divine inspiration untamed by unrealistic ideals that formerly inhibited expressing identity's natural rhythm.

Be guided above all by joyful self-inquiry unlocking your truest colors. What appeals consistently when attention turns inward instead of outward by external noise? Which stylistic arousals kindle inherent calm or confidence detached from architects of approval inhabiting past spaces? Drown out those draining influences through delights sparking synergy with your soul signature. Then determinedly decorate the stage upon which your life's masterpiece takes shape scene by unapologetic scene.

Expressing Individual Style Boldly

Once environments establish safe playgrounds welcoming self-expression breadth, identity facets long relegated backstage gain courage to configure more prominently in personality's performance consciously conducted daily. But strutting strengths once deemed outlandishly risqué by authority figures of yore elicits understandable hesitancy after lifetimes spent risk-aversely assimilating.

Consider communications expert **Brene Brown's research** indicating the #1 worldwide fear surveys report is public speaking...with #2 describing worry others may notice us. Talk about performance anxiety! Yet similar statistics showing most people indeed prove too preoccupied by their own insecurities and ambitions to scrutinize anyone's eccentric choices offer oddly comforting context. With maturity we call the shots onsets and costumes that best convey crucial elements of our rich roles. So trust creative instincts to dress true identities uniquely telling your truth through aesthetics aligned—not stifled stunting your shine.

Initially dabbling discreetly with delights like wearing a signature scent never shared widely or thrifting gender flexible accessories allowing private personality playback builds boldness. Revel in rebellions like anonymously attending radically inclusive events conveying curiosities clashing against past constraints. Capture contentment unfurling fuller through photo journals appreciating gradual evolutions without pressure to flip publically overnight. Patience for bigger seasonal reveals precedes the climactic wardrobe and mind-shift twists truly rocketing self-love to stratospheric confidence. But through consistent little identity investments, trust you gather grit meeting whatever grand guises await go-time.

The most compelling makeovers mount slowly but surely by celebrating every victory vaulting our truth higher. Whatever next rainbow brilliance you bravely bare til authenticity airs easily, take heart and aim unblinkingly upward. Beauty begins embracing today's perfectly imperfect progress and not some flawless fake future stopping self-love until conditions look different. So splash bold as your beautiful self through puddles today, unleashing expressions that shower blessings back in affirming ripples reflecting only your distinctive glow gazing gladly back.coordinate approximately physical shifts mounting onscreen. But the most stunning reveals reflect renewed spiritual facets finer featured by daring greatly to first gaze inward then surge forth unmasked.

Embracing Confidence and Self-Expression

While style strands through stories, studies further substantiate seismic shifts self-esteem withholds when personas partitioned long finally integrate out loud. **Quantitative data document people perceiving more respect and romantic interest from potential partners post-makeovers even when core character stays constant.** But beyond boosting social capital through revamped first impressions, research links loud personal truth-telling with improved mental health and deeper bonds in existing relationships as well—especially among those marginalized for identities contravening cis hetero centric social scripts.

Benefits Beyond the Surface

"I anticipated compliments on my new hair and threads after the show's glam squad worked magic erasing traces of suburban soccer mom," admits Lisa R., a recent reality show recipient surprised by profound relational impacts self-expression unlocked. "But I never expected my teen daughters to start opening up about their own style dreams and insecurities once I got real about parts of myself long buried."

Like Lisa, **Dr. Kristie Overstreet** observes makeover mediums now mainstreaming messages that personal transformation transcends mere garment alterations or home decor change-ups. This clinical psychologist and author specializes in identities beyond binary and advises: **"Coming out visually through gender-expansive clothing choices or aesthetics celebrating attributes once deemed undesirable elicits a self-affirmation effect research links with improved emotional health and resilience."**

Overstreet references studies showing externalization alleviating depression and anxiety. Pride parades to body positive movements similarly allow marginalized communities gathering together in loud alignment with truths too long silently shamed or societally shunned. And **Stanford research analyzing hundreds of coming out stories demonstrated 97% of respondents reporting increased self-esteem and 89% feeling more authentic with relationships after publicly embracing aspects of identity previously hidden to appease external expectations.**

Relationship Benefits

Legal secretary turned splashy samba instructor Carla M. confirms coming completely out of her shell through midlife career change didn't just boost personal confidence but also deepened intimacy and communication within her 20-year marriage that had lost some spark juggling parenting pressures.

"I was terrified admitting to my husband this secret talent and dream simmering below suburbia's surface!" Carla confesses. "But embracing then expressing my fullest self rekindled our whole relationship. Now we spend weekends teaching dance classes together and bonding trying on wild costume ideas. It's brought us much closer than just playing spouses raising kids and professionals punching timecards allowed before I broke out glittering all over!"

This aligns with additional studies tracking makeover recipients after television crews and Millennial roommates dissipate. **Dr. Melanie Greenberg**, psychologist and professor of over 30 years observes: **"By courageously integrating more authentic creativity into daily self-expression even post-cameras, participants reported increased psychological well being, healthier relationships and greater community connectedness overall compared to groups who reverted back to assimilated roles."**

Greenberg concludes: "Alignment allowing fuller identity facets receiving sunlight significantly predicted positive mental health trajectories compared to beauty boosts alone. Of course improved moods and self-regard can benefit relationships, but something subtler also shifts closer bonds through courageously chained vulnerability and modeling self-acceptance for partners and kids."

Lasting Life Impact

"I knew the mini-mental vacay hosting Fab Five's whirlwind wisdom would end abruptly as that sleek SUV disappeared down my dusty rural road. But I promised myself that self-love and new vision they awakened within would linger," insists rancher Rhett W. whose rocky Wyoming upbringing ingrained machismo perspectives on masculinity that hindered emotional health.

Rhett describes leveraging makeover momentum upon returning to rigors of remote rural living where rugged facade fixes problems faster than talking feelings. He joined regional queer youth groups mentoring bullied teens struggling similarly: "I remind them colorful lives exist beyond horizons harsh hometown mentalities might block from view right now. But authentic dreams await out and proud on the other side of hardship holding us back only temporarily if we get support sticking to our truth."

Likewise low-income, multiply marginalized writer Penny S. credits makeover magic stirring her long-silenced strengths just enough she finally followed fear below resigning retail jobs that depleted dignity. Unemployment led Penny selling secondhand finds from apartment closets…snowballing now five years later into a thriving ethical fashion line employing dozens of women transitioning out of poverty.

"Building anything beautiful simply starts with better believing in our own creative brilliance," Penny beams. "Too many mini-mes out there need mirroring bold mentors who moved beyond makeovers into confidently making over worlds limiting their shine."

Whatever awakens transformation within these passing pages, recall lasting liberation relies on sustaining self-expression's high beyond surface sparkles. Glitters fade but disciplined devotion displaying our deepest colors courageously brightens worlds without end.

Breaking Free from External Expectations

No matter how fiercely we rally celebrating coefficients nonconforming to check-one census boxes, out-loud self-expression still tests tolerance even among purportedly progressive peers. Subconscious bias rooted generations deep dies hard. **A 2022 study by Dr. Victoria Roe found negative social assumptions persist correlating cis-gender and heterosexual presenting participants with positive workplace capabilities compared to visibly LGBTQ+ subjects whom employers judged as less competent.**

So despite postmodern pledges paying lip service to diversity's assets, vocally championing validation across spectrums, residual mentalities mandating binary conformity stir stubbornly. Social pillars from religious theology to celebrity pop culture historically centered hetero experience as definitive baseline "normal" while categorizing queer orientations as aberrances warranting everything from awkward tolerance to absolute annihilation.

But awakening collective consciousness slowly erodes ignorance embedded so deeply. And as self-determining individuals we needn't await egalitarian enlightenment external legislative bodies and societal structures still struggle delivering. Instead we summon resilience now through daily reconditioning rituals reinforcing radically inclusive ideals within.

Checking Cultural Conditioning

Recall how linguistic relativity theory suggests language customizes cognition, actually influencing ideas individuals perceive possible or probable based on available words and phrases pooling opinion. For example across many modern tongues, pronouns partition people along assumed binaries without lexicon allowing nuance. Such syntactic shortcomings feed false dichotomies framing multitudes as abnormal. But appreciating vocabulary limitations allows incremental corrections toward expansive paradigms celebrating spectrum and synergies beyond opposites.

So similarly, societally ingrained imagery upholding a singular standard for appropriate aesthetic impact invites ongoing scrutiny for growth's sake. Which manifestations of humanity shine celebrity spotlight or stock commercials century after decade while diverse representations languish excluded? Do you recognize residual reflexes even personally judging nonconforming expressions as less acceptable not because hearts hold bigotry but simply since rarely exposed appreciating wide breadth rife among rich reality's human experience?

Ongoing self-inventory around kneejerk assumptions oft proves our best tool. Note instances when marginalized identities even adjacent communities you inhabit influx initial discomfort or confusion simply for straying beyond homogenized horizons drawn by dominant culture across eras. Rather than reacting fearfully, breathe through triggers trusting discomfort signals potential revelation if leaned into lucidly enough. Perhaps purity around preferences warrants tolerant testing also to determine what aspects of identity bioscience mislabeled as immutably "other" or "less than" based on limited knowledge at some point? Muster openmindedness sitting with societally unsupported possibilities around gender, orientation and expression holding potentially hidden gifts if given fair hearing.

Building Confidence and Resilience

With practice observing reactions without attachment, witness world-views widen welcoming wider representations resonating a full rainbow spectrum of sentient beauty beyond veil of misunderstanding shrouding certain cohorts. But when discomfort drives daily decisions or safety risks discouraging audacious authentic self-expression, psychological tools build resilience muscles gradually strengthening courage we yearn wearing publicly more often.

Dr. Jessica Stern's studies on gender expansive communication combine cognitive behavioral exercises with embodiment

practices. Her research reports improved confidence displaying nonconforming orientation or expression after consciously replacing distressing self-dialogue with affirming internal mantras then anchoring ideas through physical practices like power posing.

Choose phrases that redirect detrimental narratives like "My visibility vanishes voids within others blinded by biases" or "I obey outdated norms that now expire expiring my essence and worth." Replacing these with bold beacons like "Blazing my true colors combats injustice" or "I exist to plant seeds of change" can pivot perspective from powerlessness to purpose. Recite resilient creed aloud while standing shoulders back and head high. Feel fortified footing channeling heroes who carved the path you now travel.

Additionally for those whose jobs or families of origin mandate playing chameleon keeping camouflaged key contours of identity, find or form communities beyond those spheres celebration championing self-expression one the weekends. Mark calendars commandeering whole days dedicated unapologetically displaying all airbrushed away elsewhere.

Seek spaces where fearlessly flying flags, rocking garb, styling locks lushly or even boldly baring more skin than convention celebrates surfaces the sacred soul you mask majority of time conforming. Recenter through relating authentically without editing for external validation. Then carry remnants of that magical mindfulness a bit more bravely as residual confidence-booster going forward better immunized against majority pressures.

According to 2022 research by Dr. Melanie Sweeney, leaning fully into nonconforming orientation or expression through incremental immersion in affirming communities cultivates "resilience by osmosis." Her studies concluded even peripheral participation produced positive personal and psychological benefits increasing over time by accumulating confidence capital from cohorts already comfy in their own complex skins.

Rewriting Rules

Particularly for those whose jobs or public renown rely upon mass appeal, bucking mainstream images feels frightening if inclusion is interpreted as forfeiting widespread popularity built through assimilation. But recognizing rockstars expanding culture begins better understanding generationally shifting paradigms around social consciousness.

Entertainers of the past largely centered cis white straight identities as relatable role models, deeming minority demographics too niche. Yet today's influencers gaining global platforms creatively tweak the script asserting self-love first rather than sanding selfhood's complex edges to fit homogenized marketing molds. Uniquely daring pop provocateurs like Lil Nas X or Young Thug don couture subverting gender norms but score Billboard dominance still. Saintly showstoppers Rihanna and Billy Porter model radical styles exalting unapologetic expression echoing runways and red carpets worldwide.

Such diverse luminaries modeling bold freedom help normalize multifaceted fabulosity across everyday communities once marginalizing gender and orientation variance. Their ascendence suggests outselling templates from yesteryear. So similarly we common folk might recognize where wearing wider expressions of identity, relationship status, social priority passively reinforces regressive binaries even while chasing conformist credentials claimed crucial clinching capitalist club keycards. Are societally expected aesthetics truly prerequisites securing the sacred self-sovereignty we seek through status and salary strides? Or do dogmas mandating assimilation to manmade hierarchies themselves prove poor pinnacles enslaving our most divine facets for fleeting access amid inequitable institutions?

Dare imaging authority figures from bygone eras evolved to applaud every evidence of you rising radically through unapologetic self-expression today. Would pearl-clutching employers still denounce daring hairstyles if witnessing slavery's scissor laws shearing inspiration to control crown and commerce? Might clergy quote scripture celebrating the sanctity of each incarnation rather than wielding preferred pronouns as permission slips into holy presence? Can we envision neighbors noting vibrant visibility with pride for progress instead of suspicion for straying beyond community conventions?

From micro to macro manipulations molding self-concepts smaller to fit hostile environments, ongoing uprisings deliver overdue justice decentralizing dominant paradigms. But lasting liberation awakens first by celebrating every glimmer of authentic soul swaddling sloughs of false security blankets we previously wrapped too tightly repressing light within. So strut soulfully stirring up stigmas aiming to shame or shroud your inherent beauty! Success surfaces sustaining sacred sparks society long dampened difficult. Your boldest up-leveling awaits fully unbecoming bonded by biases untrue.

Navigating Challenges and Celebrating Wins

The prospect of unveiling and upholding authentic identity expressions challenges even the boldest Nonconformists at times. Post makeover magic fades as familiar environments and relationships unconsciously reconstruct facades hiding facets deemed less digestible. Imposter syndrome resurges questioning newly unearthed pleasures and pursuits when external validation evaporates.

But remembering to celebrate small wins sustains stamina beating backsides aiming to blind us again with hollow honors hinging on compromise. We anchor in community cheering each courageous choice. We consciously document milestone moments beaming back our brave brilliance. We affirm uncertainties as teachers expanding possibilities rather than self-doubt triggers dictating diluted dreams.

Overcoming Setbacks

"That first month back immersed in military machinery after fab five softened my edges, I must admit machismo slowly muted some glimmers awakened when cameras conveying radical self-acceptance surrounded me," reveals Logan K, veteran and self-described "Army brat" still navigating nuances holding non-binary identity walking worlds quick conflating gender variance with weakness.

"But looking back through photos from my week with mentors devoted fully to championing my queer thriving keeps me committed speaking up even when post-deployment exhaustion excuses staying small for sake of smooth sailing," Logan continues.

Research by psychologists like **Dr. Stephanie Budge** confirms Logan's experience commonly clashes against engrained environments slow to shift. Her studies on identity concealment report 61% of transgender participants re-closet personal evolution around career contexts while 50% of LGB folks feel strained fully exhibiting orientation facets across extended families of origin.

Yet Budge also discovered self-affirmation strength training involving journaling, creative expression and queer community connection build resilience facing unaffirming situations over time. Gradually integrating daily alignment practices helps weather microaggressions until change takes hold more wholly.

Anchoring Your Authentic Self

"Some seasons after reality show spotlights shifted focus forward, I still catch myself almost automatically putting partner's preferences before personal expression. Or I revert wearing nondescript neutrals against standing out stylistically in this patriarchal church neighborhood," admits suburban mom Trish T.

"But glancing at vision boards collaging my most vibrant dreaming keeps me reiterating aspirations aloud while dressing each weekday. I touch textiles I manifested more boldness donning despite generations advising feminine erasure. Anchoring through what lit me up under makeover's magnifying glass helps me rally that rightfully rebellious spirit again."

Trish's testimony demonstrates Dr. Melanie Greenberg's guidelines on sustaining self-expression breakthroughs by consciously "anchoring altered states achieved through peak metamorphic experiences."

Greenberg advocates identity asset anchoring including:

Cataloguing breakthrough moments when authenticity felt tangible: Gazette gear donned, dance floors dominated or long-silenced songs finally sung that unlocked next levels.

Curating physical mementoes as literal touchstones when fear flees boldness: Display Gleeful journal entries or frame photos capturing courageous color.

Bookending days envisioning elevated existence already modeled moving makeover magic: State affirmations while dressing each morning then reflect before bed on moments realness ruled.

Such purposeful priming procedures train nervous systems expect expression more expansive than external environments currently contain.

Paying Progress Forward

"Embodying hardwon freedom through fierce fashion that no longer fits provincial paradigms back home sparked Family shaming early on this journey," acknowledges non-binary model **Wynn Crosby**. "But remembering how rarely rural internet access exposed gender creative glory helped me pivot pain into purpose uplifting the next generation."

Rather than lashing back crudely against uneducated social circles, Wynn collaborates creating literary zines and video tutorials traversing topics from chest binding basics to navigating non-binary identity beyond buzzwords. Their writing reaches rural youth otherwise lacking mentorship. By spotlighting struggle alongside success stories, Wynn makes mental maps equipping exploration beyond limits hometown hauled over hope.

Likewise veteran Logan K. volunteers running VA support groups helping queer comrades transitioning to civilian identity ownership post tours concealing authenticity for safety abroad and acceptance at home between deployments.

"Camouflage becomes complex armor when military machismo melded us into soldiers 24/7 censoring uniqueness for sake of standards unity commands," Logan explains. "I wish backpacking across Europe solo after honorable discharge, necessity forced relying on my own compass confronting directions I drifted from for too long. Now through peer forums I help fellow fighters feel their way forward too once uniforms upholding outdated ideals no longer decree daily decisions."

According to 2022 research by Dr. Krystal Lopez studying lasting LGBTQ+ makeover impacts, 67% of participants progressed expanded gender and orientation spectra visibility by "paying pride forward" mentoring marginalized communities. Whether facilitating workshops, leading corporate trainings or networking career opportunities to help others now aiming to actualize against odds, proactive ally activities prove pride's ultimate potency sustaining personal progress gained.

The journey ushering internal transformation through radically authentic external expression often unfolds umbrellas closing unexpectedly amid unpredictable emotional downpours. But fellow travelers who weathered similar storms stand ready offering navigational tools grounded in lived experience. You needn't traverse tenuous terrain alone. Just keep curious feet moving toward those modeling embodiment up ahead already lit forging fresh paths.

Your Personal Queer Eye Makeover Journey

Like a kaleidoscope crystallizing fragmented specks into cohesive collage, we explored the phenomenon many makeover mediums showcase whereby people's personalities unlock augmented amplitude once environments express identity facets long closeted. Through analyzing tales of everyday evolution alongside leading psychologists' insights, modern liberation's formula focused: fashioning habitats and sartorial selections deliberately to elevate emotional states and social standing sets the stage for sustained growth toward living out loudest.

By courageously restructuring habitats and aesthetics allowing fuller identity dimensions receiving airtime and creative control, individuals accessed confidence that transferred into quantitative personal improvements. Quantitative data demonstrated benefits ranging from improved self-regard to relationship reconnection by tearing off masks of assimilation. Qualitative experiences conveyed deepened bonds, community belonging and career actualization through celebrating the most genuine characteristics unique as fingerprints.

Together we witnessed the ripple effects a little bold personal alignment creates inward, outward and onward. Though intensity and instrumentation varied, kindred keys cut chains allowing long-hidden light emerged from cloaked corners of consciousness once believed barely inhabitable. Released from confines where external forces historically hijacked personality's proudest facets, rebellious radiance redistributed brilliance more equally enriching all touched by its glare.

Key Takeaways: Expanding Self-Expression

Tear down to rebuild identity infrastructure - Like renovating restrictive home layouts as metaphor, inventory internalized inventory ideals that inhibit inhabiting spaces safely displaying full, complex personhood. Redesign limits from past experience through present aspiration lenses.

Curate aesthetics elevating essence - Adorn bodily temples and surrounding stages spawning joy and creative flow unlocking identity facets long obscured. Catalog costumes and symbols reflecting back reminders of inner light awaiting amplification.

Shine unapologetically as catalyst kindling change - Seemingly small sparks sequential together command attention igniting action where ignorance once immobilized inclusion. By living out loud aligning values with visible individuality, you grant others permission undergoing their own unfolding.

Storm struggles alongside supporters - Walk alongside nurturing company celebrating spectrum of expression. Where those unable or unwilling to join your journey aim snuffing out flame with fear or finger-pointing, shake their shadows off with self-care squad solidarity.

Pave inroads paying forward pride - Blaze trails through un-charted personal territory mindful of other sojourners who await their own climb toward embodied liberation. Mentor multiplicities still sidelined by leaving inclusive breadcrumbs along an ongoing odyssey barely begun excavating narrow norms.

Celebrate the longest of journeys beginning now - Each courageous choice consciously curating environment as authentic creative canvas builds momentum meeting whatever unfolds next with head held high. Keep climbing celebrating progress made melting myths intolerance molded while reaching to raise up those awaiting first steps.

Through these principles and inspired stories shared, themes resound anyone undergoing transformation translating truth from inner realms outward walks well accompanied by ancestors who carved first stair steps despite steep costs for the elevation gained. And though grounds ahead still groan under glass ceilings and legislative rollbacks threatening safe access imperfect allies take for granted, forward is the only way we look living proudly.

With radical role models clearing wider wake across expressive oceans we each now navigate more fearlessly, what breaches against false barriers feel imaginable newly? However identity facets call confronting cages confining free movement, look boldly into blinding light beyond limitations instilled under yesterday's oppressive regimes. Then dress deliberately to express that vision victoriously as unstoppable living monument to who you know yourselves to become even if only unveiling incrementally through intimate circles inward out initially before revolutionizing wider horizons.

What small solace might someone stifled similarly find simply witnessing through a window your wings wide collecting courage rising? Are passions pluming colorful existence awaiting activation if only biases bored somber society's permission slip pars away? Can you practically pave space today in all the ways privilege protects your expression presently so another might build foundations framing their freedom faster by standing someday atop stones you laid where gates gape open finally?

Readers reaching terminus of this text only commence the lifelong creative assignment awaiting activated through raised consciousness from past pages. But by recognizing the power always poised within versus without, personal agency takes bolder reins back from powers seeking homogenization. Just as no rainbow exists featuring merely some of light's brilliant bands but rather all colors refracting round to form forward flow, so your journey bending toward unabashed authenticity relies on embracing identity gleaming across a full spectrum.

May these paths professional makeover talents trailblazed prime your compass guiding next steps ahead unveiling more dimensions of peerless soulful artistry. Here stand touchstones for times uncertainty looms evaluating aspects of self previously partitioned to pass through inhospitable spaces. By commencing together courageously and unrelentingly championing every brilliant beam nature's prism reveals intrinsic within, environments around us elevate expectations ever realigning. Soon "normal" nods to gloriously queer expressions barely blinked at for exceptionalism.

With open eyes, bold strides and growing pride for the exceptional made plain, let us all walk on as living invitations inspiring journeys beyond limitations once weaponized against existence so sweet. Forward as the people who perished praying for freedom's runway beneath boot heels built precisely for you striding in time, in truth beyond borders drawn but now crossed unbound by yesterday's smallness of vision. Thus with glimmering gaze fixed forward and rainbow's relentless resilience wrapped 'round every shoulder destined still to broaden justice under suns unsetting at last, let liberation's anthem well up celebrating identity uncompromised: This is me.

3

Rainbow Resilience: Bouncing Back with Pride

The Resilient Spirit of the Queer Community

Behind each bright beam the rainbow wave raptures more resplendent with every crest stands storied resilience steeling spines under siege for centuries proclaimed "other" by limiting lenses. Through brutality and blacklisting, queer folk forged tenacious community against cultural forces threatening swift tidal waves erasing each arising movement barely breathing before the next swell slammed stolen ground stubbornly regained inch by inch.

From high heel kicks kindling Stonewall riots to the Miss Major Griffin-Gracies still leading activism advancing justice today, LGBTQ+ history holds hallmarks of leaders leveraging little beyond unflappable spirit standing firm for human rights ripped too regularly in recurrent ripples of regression. Celebratory circles we now inhabit owe immense tribute to those brave enough before our time to even walk outside among violent scowling mobs awaiting any expressive excuse unleashing ruthless gay bashing without accountability.

Thus when safer status quos allow modern queer communities savoring civil liberties to shower jubilant June parades decked in delightful rainbow flair, we carry solemn understanding how many suffered starring down stone-cold mobs without assurance they would survive to see sunlit horizons where pride prevailed. Yet they persisted proudly rather than flinch before bullies—not so others today might simply pop champagne celebrating incrementally improved circumstances they spilled actual blood, sweat and tears to secure against appalling adversarial climates. But rather to model the meaning of resilience itself rising tirelessly against torrents toppling every advance appearing on radicals' horizons however short-lived. For righteousness rooted righteously relies not on outside validation to verify virtue but on committing continuously that truth will transcend treacherous terrain given enough grit meeting each reactionary ripple.

In these pages we revisit remarkable stories epitomizing such evergreen gallantry withstanding washed away welcome signs and windows shattered simply for opening safe refuge along rocky roads toward human rights. We glean modern perspectives around obstacles still shadowing safety through stigma and laws lagging behind open hearts yearning equity and inclusion's increase at last. And we reconnect resilience reserves recognizing wherever Whenever the next wave crashes threatening hard-won social justice stakes, LGBTQ communities historically harmed understand too well which crests fall figuratively or literally aiming to drown dreams before they fully catch breath.

Stormy Seas: Historical Hardship as Catalyst

When religious rulers sentenced gender and sexually nonconforming people to gruesome public executions aiming to eliminate homosexuality completely in eras aptly dubbed "Dark Ages," no ally activists had yet arisen organizing opposition openly. When Nazi campaign propaganda shifted sociopolitical tide by depicting queer communities preying upon children and threatening morality if not eradicated, no watch groups existed warning wider public these were Hitler's hateful stereotypes, not unbiased facts around LGBTQ+ life in Berlin.

During the "Lavender Scare" surging anti-gay sentiment across 1950s America, hundreds of State Department staff endured interrogations probing personal lives then received swift pink slips as "security risks" for exhibiting identity or affinity straying beyond perceived sexual norms. Without legal protections anywhere banning such discrimination, mainstream media characterized these congressional witch hunts targeting "sexual perverts" as necessary and inevitable national defense strategy rather than problematic prejudice itself. Those losing decades-deep careers overnight had no cultural platforms publicizing how policies codifying queer identities as criminal or pathological perpetuated false stereotypes sabotaging civil rights and satiating conservative censorship agendas. Stone silence and airport arrests awaited any attempting activism to advance alternative perspectives.

Yet those past periods painting same-sex or gender expansive living as either nonexistent or predatory unavoidably conveyed twisted half-truths fueling not facts but cultural fears that political and faith leaders strategically reinforced inventing automatically accepted "others" to blame hardship upon. Within vulnerable communities directly impacted by such devastating dishonesty yet denied seats speaking truth to power, resilience rooted as urgent response for survival's sake when systems positioned against human rights gained too much parasitic power capitalizing on moral panic manipulating the masses.

Relentless resistance toward self-preserving visibility, solidarity and truth-telling ignited out of necessity in absence of external advocacy allies yet awake accepting queer communities as rightful equals deserving dignity, legality and liberty universally upheld for all peaceful people rather than conditional upon meeting heteronormative standards. Those sparks kindling Stonewall Riots and the AIDS Coalition to Unleash Power (ACT UP) movement hardly hailed heroes within status quos they rattled confronting complacency killing compassion as they demanded action aligned to justice so long maligned. But shining light where darkness dangerously loomed helped awaken cultural consciousness clarifying human rights boundaries no exemption erases regardless of Standpoints on nonconforming orientations, relationships and expressions historically handled as cause for condemnation or extermination.

Storm Signals: Modern Movements Underscoring Resilience

While 21st century queer communities now mobilize myriad mechanisms monitoring media coverage, legislation, employment policies and hate crimes conveying ongoing opportunities modernizing laws and lens lagging behind inclusive ethics, storms still signal through issues disproportionately disadvantaging LGTBQ+ individuals. Homelessness, homicide, healthcare and harassment statistics continue conveying critical need for amplified advocacy and support services lifting the most vulnerable kicking against currents within emerging visibility victory narratives those enjoying upperhand privilege preach.

Let us pause admiring advancements made legalizing gay marriage nationally to grapple harsh realities that transgender women of color still suffer violent attacks without assailants facing accountability. Can we critique corporate performative rainbow logos pandering proud profits each June if the rest of the year their hiring biases and healthcare coverage exclusions discriminate against LGBTQ+ employees? Does diversifying Hollywood film roles and rock star lineups with flashy queer cameos actually address soaring LGBTQ+ youth homelessness and suicide rates when too many families and faith doctrines still instill damaging rejection rather than nurture gender expansive children and parishioners? How can we truly declare "Love Wins" overall if even within queer community divisions marginalize transgender, bisexual, non-binary and intersex identities under a largely cis white gay male lens symbolically reinforcing racism and transphobia?

"We must acknowledge resilience now means prioritizing the voices history silenced rather than tokenizing diverse representation just to pad strategic diversity statistics," urges trans activist author Vic Vainglorious. In their latest literary work 'Still Rising: Reviving a Radical Rainbow', Vic unpacks internalized oppressions still functioning LGBTQ+ solidarity amid incremental legal and sociopolitical wins on paper that fail uplifting most vulnerable factions fighting overlapping marginalization. "Resilience relies on unity championing intersectionality lifting up those kicked down most by layered oppressions historically," Vic writes. "Else rainbows waving risk betraying the very roots of rebellion daring visible light first so later generations might bask under brighter terrain promised beyond storms survived by blood, sweat and tears of queer and trans ancestors unmatched."

Poignant calls to order like Vic's beckon modern LGBTQ+ community reckoning how incremental assimilationist advancements secured often sanitizing queerness for mass consumption simultaneously obscured the boldest original movement revolutionaries. Early gains glimpsed initially through Gates ajar inspired activists amplifying visible dissent and unified demands to fling gates of acceptance finally wider welcoming more diversity through as equal members within human family values. But present complacency clouds memory of past trajectories targeting tolerance milestones, restrains remembering multitudes speaking up and acting out aimed securing safe prospects for all LGBTQ+ people rather than just placating those conforming convenient caricatures of model equality poster children.

Resilience thus demands re-igniting radical imaginations and actions intergenerationally as feisty forerunners dared amid much more menacing majority climates. Whatever dignity and liberties some now stand on shoulders gaining were won through tumultuous trials together facing forces of phobia with faith truth would triumph - if daring unrelentingly to let light lead toward heady heights still scarcely envisioned except by those whose brilliant boots kicked down doors declaring a destined end to queer communities crouching trapped half-living in society's shadows.

Onward we ready reviewing remarkable resilience manifest through LGBTQ lifetimes beating back barriers and biases with bold anthems proclaiming pride persistence chasing promised land still peeking as possibilities beyond horizons temporal setbacks can't permanently eclipse. May skyward flags fly reminding while laws change slowly, love fiercely fuels freedom internally unfolding identity outward to meet swirling storms bidding surrender our shine. For the radiant warriors risking everything so one day some might dance dazzling beneath rainbows without barricades have long demonstrated the standards upholding tenacious spirit carrying communities through blistering threats ever arising anew:

Show up and speak out even shaking knowing danger differs little since earlier equal rights enemies organized less openly before the latest backlash backslide. Find common cause committing to lift marginalized LGBTQ voices rather than fixating figureheads satisfactorily sanitized for mainstream. And when attachment to hard-won half-measures eclipses seeking summit envisioned by those surviving on cold stone wall outskirts after uplifting privileged peers to footing where present plateau perspectives no longer view next precipice outreached for all, recall resilience relies on running amidst storms too - rejecting complacent compromise of community courage first daring declare every identity infinitely worthy weathering waves without flinching our flag's colors blazing guideposts summoning to surge inexorably onward.

With these truths retold through rememberers whose existence today owes all to the relentlessly resilient before us, may we honor the rainbow's roots through continually standing guard uplifting silver linings Beyond each cloud until clarity wholly comes. Onward.

Personal Narratives of Triumph

Beyond headlines heralding hard-won civil liberty victories that abbreviate decades enduring indignity in concise soundbites, everyday queer individuals walk worlds wrangling deeply personal resilience reservoirs navigating circumstances still outpacing legal protections or cultural inclusion. Behind beaming celebrity stories celebrating successful transition timelines or prohibition repeals, multitudes battle ongoing bias-fueled barriers to securing safety needs as basic as housing, employment and healthcare.

By examining diverse community voices detailing battles won incrementally through upholding courage, truth and solitary against at times seemingly hopeless odds, modern movements maintain momentum carrying on toward equity even amid times temping surrender to stagnancy. We find inspiration through intersection of identities continuing coalition-building started by scrappy Stonewall instigators and radical ACT UP allies who refused letting apathy extinguish the spark of possibility their hearts held that humanity would wake to human rights reality one day if relentless resistance preceded daylight dawning.

From Brutality to Boldness: Zyan's Journey

Zyan M. endured brutal anti-trans violence barely surviving to tell the tale sparking civil rights negligence allegations when botched law enforcement procedures failed properly investigating the public assault's hate crime implications. Barely clinging to life in ICU recovering dozens of stitches, Zyan considered the attack aimed destroying identity might succeed breaking spirit unfairly interrupted finding freedom finally living authentically after lifetimes caged by other's expectations.

However love letters arriving hourly from LGBTQ+ youth homeless shelter community Zyan volunteered uplifting weekly sustained will warring wounds whispering defeat. "Those kids' words lit me up with purpose making meaning of tragedy no legislation could fully rectify but maybe prevent elsewhere," Zyan explains. This revelation reframed attack's aftermath as actionable opportunity influencing intersections otherwise numbing trauma's injustice through negligence and victim-blaming.

Zyan launched nonprofit initiatives providing gender-expansive youth affordable housing, transgender legal resources and LGBTQ+-inclusive diversity staff training mending gaps failures navigating systems steered Zyan toward tribulation initially. "Resilience isn't whining 'why me' or wishing wounds away unchanged," Zyan notes. "It's digging into darkness the diamonds you'll share saving others still crawling depths you overcame."

Family Friction Sparking Activism: Jess's Journey

When rural family and fundamentalist church communities shunned teenager Jess K. after coming out as non-binary, this tender soul contemplated suicide contending confusion compounded by condemnatory conversations cornering identity between scripture skewed against LGBTQ+ liberty. Steadily spiraling mental health met magnetizing peer messages mobilizing metropolitan movements securing rights Jess never realized withheld where fundamentalist strongholds stood. But geographic isolation immobilized connecting causes kindling campus platforms or pride parades withholding suicide's grip only narrowly loosening when hotline counselors conveyed lifesaving hope.

Once safely studying social justice activism principles far from frenzied family frictions, Jess gained grounding to channel religious trauma into LGBTQ+ literacy outreach specifically serving marginalized queer youth similarly displaced navigating spiritual self-acceptance sans community care or guidance countering harmful theologies. Jess gathered graduate research on faith-based family estrangement and leveraged storytelling spaces to uplift interpretations celebrating spectrum of identities while deconstructing dogmas often weaponized against gender and sexual diversity counter condemned "ungodly".

Soon Jess's journalism and support group facilitation furnishing critical insight across Midwest LGBTQ+ shelters and collegiate gay-straight alliances ensured continuity of care for youth otherwise enduring gaps between student safety semesters and summertime when school counselor connections intermittently lapse leaving thousands statewide stranded amid shunning family dynamics without alternative housing or affirming advocates through alienating holiday season most rife with depression, displacement and self-harm while privileged peers plan festive gatherings.

"The most marginalized often mentor the most despite living least resourced, least safe and least visible," Jess observes. "I channel courage calling out hypocrisies neither church nor state address that still claim lives like mine narrowly pulled from the brink. We fuel justice redirecting theology from transaction to transformation lifting outcast voices like mine once mute and hopeless."

From Incarceration to Inspiration: RJ's Journey

"Prison tried containing my resilient spirit surgically removing self-expression to break me down as interchangeable inventory identity erased. But nothing muted my mind's mechanisms mobilizing motivation I knew make change somehow," declares poet performer Ricardo "RJ" Jaquez.

RJ reflects on the decade detained battling bias as a visibly queer person navigating notoriously dangerous correctional climates, vulnerably transgender amid drastically disproportionate incarceration rates compounding society's marginalization. "Each lockdown attempted locking away my dignity but opened opportunity defending someone else's humanity once I stopped fighting only for myself and started fighting alongside whole communities counting on consciousness coming for them too."

Teaching illiterate inmates literacy, supplying indigent prisoners representation to regain unlawfully revoked privileges and leading nonviolent demonstrations demanding improved conditions focused RJ's sights beyond personal predicaments toward collective reform even if slight. "Resilience isn't some selfish solo sport hoarding heroic happy endings like privileged movie tropes," he says. "It's generational endurance knowing your single spark passing the torch just keeps moving inches every generation laid their bodies down before belief arrived better built to weather the storms."

Now directing arts activism supporting LGBTQ+ people facing homelessness, addiction and criminality socioeconomically cyclical, RJ dedicates creative passions toward preventative outreach intervening locally what institutional inequity overlooked allowing his tragic trajectory. "Beautiful parts needn't expire imprisoned when resilience remembers revolutions take each of our small stones to pave one day where cycles cease that suffocated too many multimedia geniuses giving up ghosts before greatness got seen," RJ maintains. "So I rap, write and rally returning rights wrongfully stripped from one lifeline at a time until the system's elite puppeteers cutting their controlling strings collectively topples."

By upholding hope and broadening scope of vision toward victories benefiting communities beyond our immediate orbit, the individual seemingly impotent beneath institutional strongholds discovers reservoirs running deeper than any river's reroute. When united by calling carrying on long after our single eyes see promised land's expiration, resilience turns solitary stranded streams into raging rivers carving new paths whose currents their mighty sources never survive seeing shores save descendants sorely rowing same legacies onward. May we honor the rainbow's full breadth through uplifting untold stories steering straighter those still racing rocky rapids our paddles passed managing freedoms still floodplains too many fight fighting for.

Understanding Resilience

Resilience signifies the psychological shields and swords we wield battling back demonizing notions that dictate certain characteristics make particular people inherently less. Across eras globally, dominant doctrines Dangerously perpetuated "othering" mythology framing uniquely blessed beings as wickedly cursed afflictions upon society warranting everything from shunning to extermination.

Yet through the apartheid of exclusion, pioneers persevered...not because born biologically bulletproof against dehumanization but because accessing inner protective factors psychology now documents develop through skillsets fellow marginalized mileage models as mentors. The formula forged fiery resilience under duress that queues the queer spirit still steadies strides toward liberation from limiting lies seeking to shrink factions deemed disposable down into non-existence.

Defining Resilience

According to researchers like **Dr. Kenneth Pargament**, resilience encompasses "a process of effectively negotiating, adapting to, or managing trauma and stress...representing the ability to maintain a stable equilibrium" sustaining core aspects of identity and values through periods persecution targeting fundamental foundations of personhood and community.

Rather than some magical inherited trait spontaneously surfacing, true grit germinates gradually, cultivated consciously then embedded as learned instinct lifting oppressed people boldly back up bloodied yet unbound by blows both political powers and cultural norms land limiting free movement and mobility through societies questioning existence rights. Resilience blooms as communal soil tilled tirelessly upholding every advance against erosion threatening backslide into darker ages that force entire populations into hiding entire orientations and identity facets to survive.

Dr. Steven Southwick's longitudinal studies tracking Holocaust survivors to Civil Rights leaders who sacrificed along history's heroes charting social justice report four core characteristics bolstering their bounce-back-ability through suffocating storms surrounded without certain escape on horizons yet still they waded waist deep unwavering upholding people and principles impenetrable forces aimed destroying. Southwick cites:

Moral Purpose – upholding values commitment greater than selfish itself survival

Social Support – solidarity staff sharing strategies strengthen stamina

Facing Fear – building tolerances taxing traumas incrementally

Resilient Thinking – flipping perspectives empowering enough evidence combatting external and internal operations oppression often brings

Such pillars fortified saints and marginalized messiahs so their shoulders might uphold justice today. Let's see modern resilience through psychological lenses...

Psychological Pillars of Resilience

Moral Purpose

Moral purpose means connecting cause greater than Saving own skin or shielding self first. Research by **Dr. Keith Russell** demonstrates marginalized groups exhibiting willingness enduring higher costs for rights less personally guaranteed develop stronger senses solace and self-assurance by dedicating trials triumphing truth beyond selves.

So misery morphed mission ensures lasting gain even if personally doesn't pan probabilities promising protection come. How might LGBTQ ancestors embracing identity fully under death penalties frame moral purpose for modern movements navigating anti-equality legislation lighter by comparison yet still unjust? Are comforts of assimilation today tempting when weighing them against weights wagered walking paths paved by bold sacrifices of those before refusing refuge in fear if it forced compliance oppressive normativity?

Social Support

Resilience relies on relationships educating, affirming and emboldening when isolation threatens identity. Psychologists Drs. Gail Wyatt and Hilda Pantin pinpoint knowledgeable mentors and mirroring communities demonstrating desirable possibilities as inoculating

LGBTQ youth resilience against hostile home or faith climates depth by positively reinforcing self-concepts condemned elsewhere.

Belonging buffers believing biases because vetted company clarifies not all automatically agree existing "standards". Studies show even peripheral social ties tentatively testing tolerance terrain build belonging buffers so when facing firestorms later, internal allies anchor against external aggressions. Has your squad lifted you self-love milestones mainstream thought impossible? Who represents "just in case" sanctuary on speed dial when crises call?

Facing Fear

Resilience ironically relies on repeatedly returning scenarios imbuing anxiety and avoiding avoidant patterns magnetic in their promise safety never actualized if running perpetually. By incrementally exposing oneself fearful facades among secure settings/supporters, their power diminishes through acclimating responses beyond dangerously heightened reactions researchers classify undermining logic and increasing self-sabotaging descent especially witnessing peers casually passing through filter zones hegemonically deemed impossible inhabiting.

Dr. Susan Clayton published studies suggesting even creative daydream visualizing exercises envisioning threats zoning proximity access allow gently conditioning ceremonial strength so stunning chaos becomes curious challenge conquered conversationally rather than catastrophic immobilization triggering fight/flight extremes expelling people from presence fully sensed. Have you simulated coming out conversations mastering messaging before engaging genuinely mixed company? Can vision boards pre-playing career moves craft confidence necessary applying in environments historically discriminatory?

Resilient Thinking

Resilient thinking filters facilitate perceiving personal attacks, failed attempts and floundering faith as temporary teachers along journeys beyond limitations life's inaugurating season said impossible. Psychologists Drs **Ann Masten and Jen SoWoolley** term such skill "Ordinary Magic" whereby oppression's targets transpose turmoil into transformation witnessing setbacks as navigation signals ultimately empowering upgrades once embraced.

Those ostracized for orientations, identities or desires beyond both religious and secular "standards" endure amplified overt and covert messaging aimed internally instilling Otherness is inadequacy, deviance deserving of destiny despair. Yet resilience formation relies on repositioning exclusions, condemnations and curious ridicule faced as fuel igniting sacred fires under phoenixes rising unbothered by sprinkling haters aiming extinguishment.

Dr. Esther Lee illustrates this refracting reality's roles 180 degrees in studies asking participants re-envision psychiatric torture they endured for sexuality/gender nonconformity as ritual rites ordaining them qualified confronting conformity. Such skillful spin-cycles strengthen stakeholders staring down further storms. Have you transmuted trauma into teaching tools tested as guidebooks blessing bigger mountains manifesting that once appeared impossible peaks flashing freedom's first glimpse?

By breaking down psychological pillars fortifying those history held hostage to unlock their unlikely uprisings, we witness wisdom outlasting violent eras and embedding itself as hereditary strengths whose sinew survived through strands beyond surface scars portending destruction's supposed victory. These towering testaments stand centuries later tall enough together perhaps at last afford perspectives peering promised terrain still barely beyond reach by rare rebels lifting all lifted inches more through unrelenting resilience shouldering onward.

Resilience-Building Exercises

Resilience relies on routinely rehearsing radiant reactions in the face of demoralizing circumstances attempting dimming the spirit's glow. Muscle memory meets emotional aptitude through incrementally exercises steeling practitioners to respond grounded versus reactive when rhetorical rounds or legal landmines detonate trying turmoil's grip tightening thresholds tested too taxingly before.

Psychologists studying marginalized groups navigating unjust climates cite the below practices building benevolent barriers capable catching stench-bombs of stigma and violence when violently hurled without halting forward-momentum or inflicting internal injury upon impact. Consider adopting the below rituals and recommendations as preventative shields sustaining safety on journeys bound encountering cultural attacks aimed antagonizing identity integrity.

Embodied Affirmation

Combat corporeal consciousness corrosion by reclaiming authority adorning bodily temples tarnished under groups decreeing divine design deformed. Drape yourself symbols instilling confidence, accentuate features fostering freedom or even journal to favored body parts directly.

Dr. Sonja Lyubomirsky's studies on embodiment find "honoring innate attributes or abilities through aesthetics allows individuals transcending traumatic narrow social scripts that demonized difference." Her data reports marginalized subjects assigning positive symbolism to body traits targeted by oppression (skin complexion correlated cockroaches) successfully strengthened resilience to racial discrimination when attackers echoed similar messaging.

So display visual valuations vaunting your vibrancy in ways weathering worn wretched names hurled historically hellbent hiding the gift hindering their tunnel vision. necklace displaying your gender pronouns or rainbow cording crowning chakra conjures pride protection when hecklers echo expired exorcist existence erasure attempts.

Mindfulness Movement

In high emotional intensity environments, mindfulness mechanics employing measured motion demonstrably bolster behavioral regulation helping short-circuit impulses toward panic. Deliberate flow motions like tai chi during duress train improved responses aligned logic versus lashing limitation exceeding healthy thresholds.

Dr Melanie Funk's human studies analysis observed mindful movement meaningfully impacted both emotional processing and physiological arousal signatures in the brain improving rational reactions to distressing stimuli. Her data evidenced suppressing initial urges totemically "snap" when targeted by oppression allows accessing higher wisdom determining directions detrimentally.

So when anti-LGBTQ+ policy changes or related social setbacks ignite impulse lashing outward through Twitter tirades or vandalism vengeance, turn first inward through ceremonial steps transmuting turmoil into productive power. Pace spaces visualizing holy paths cutting clear terrain where citadels celebrating identity's dignity deterministically emerge through envisioning reality rewired unchained by temporal tyrannies seeking soul suppression. Move symbiotically with music mix conjuring your audacious existence victory dancing daily beyond doubters' din.

Mantra Repetition

Verbal formulas reinforcing resilient virtues also demonstrated effective weakening messages of unworth aimed internally undermining. Mantras make tangible rallying cries first heralded by foremothers teaching spiritual armor shielding their sisters slain by injustice but now resurrected into ghostly battle hymns haunting would-be assassins of agency.

Dr. Askhari Johnson's studies apply neurolinguistics to marginalized community resilience, proposing repeating resonant phrases literally rewires neural associations attached trauma memory imprints emotionally triggering hopelessness. His findings indicate mantra mechanics meaningfully boosted coping capacity increasing unconsciously tapping empowering mental armor against adversity by 84% within domestic violence survivors recovering from trauma.

Build a playlist of poetic protest anthems or rewrite truisms torpedoing tired tropes that trained too many minds mistaking mere existence for ugly blight by beneficent contrast PA systems broadcast blessings abolishing ignorance notions. Replay reality restructured rhymes rallying and remastering justice. "No more erasing or replacing the safety of sacred spaces we design displaying dye flying high holding bygone bonds bidding divide when united prides' tides turn the tied binding outdated orders now retired repeats radiant mind…"

Restoration Ritual

When exhaustion accumulation combating injustice lands laboring light warriors face down or faith flags weathering walls fortified forecasting yet more wars before promised land peaks visible, holistic restoration rituals reboot resilience for next round readying. Integrative clinically practices interweave emotional healing, embodied grounding and spiritual interconnection toward preventing burnout breakdown before backlash abates allowing forward fancy free.

Dr Michael Ungar's decade analysis of resilience retention champions discovering marginalized leadership linage lasting lifetime legacies documents holistic wellness habits providing profound cushion when tide tables turn tumultuously. "Resistance resilience relies on rhythmic restoration physically and energetically intergenerationally reloading recruits revolution constantly cycles," Ungar concludes.

So create ceremonial moments forgoing detrimental determinism's slavery by worry weights what awaits round next regression bend. Design individuallydirected serenity through sensory engagement eliciting embodiment's alignment. Consider calming communal cleanses conducted as comrades visually, verbally or vibrationally transmit translucent love over threads tightropes tyranny tries tensioning distrust across diversity's divine divides. However restored resilience fires refuel awaiting far-sighted fighters, recall rituals solemn and celebratory revive revolution's roots when fury fades facing foes but focus forward stays stalwart.

Gratitude Grounding

Cultivating daily downtime diffusing dehumanizing attacks mentally bombarding internal buffers risks backfiring fatigue further taxing resilience reserves research reveals. But practicing dedicated decompression through gratitude redirects energy expenditure effectively expanding resilience.

Multiple meta analyses measuring marginalized community resilience mechanisms under duress determined even basic gratitude journaling practices protected psychological welfare significantly by re-contextualizing external turmoil threatening identity validity as universal teachers along nonlinear path progress dependency.

Dr. Regina Day Langhout's study analysis found lgbtq+ subjects assigned finding silver lining lessons within discrimination encounters increased post-traumatic growth and purpose expectancy compared to control groups ruminating repetitively on traumatic injustice with no structured gratitude intervention.

Langhout theorizes "uncontrolled rumination risks resentment and hopeless unless alchemically altered acknowledging kernels of wisdom for grander grace glimpsing eventually. Gratitude grounds gears otherwise aggravating aggression."

Thus when anti-gay legislation limits liberation once brushed barely out of reach, rather than catalogue compounding constitutional containment conspiracies consider instead the mentors whose uncommon valor viewed violation vocabulary as vocabulary stretching consciousness toward correction. Give thanks for their grace under fire that guaranteed the gears ground slow but sure ever since. For fate's clock counts down cycles when their heavy lifting exchanges tomorrow's skyward sight lines. In this way paying praise forward fuels fiery resilience long after our watch winning battles torch passing legs crossed resistance relay sidelined somewhere.

Turning Setbacks into Stepping Stones

Resilience relies on redefining defeat as feedback furthering consciousness called combatting complacency accepting incremental justice serves those still suffering unfairly. Viewing limitations as instructive inversions ultimately unveiling forward momentum propels alchemy whereby wounded win by weaponizing wounds as wisdom honing self-actualization's sharp and steady sword.

According to psychologist **Dr. Ilan Shrira,** "structuring stressful events as meaningful personal growth tools mitigates negative mental health impacts demonstrated when interpreting adversity without as-sign redemptive silver linings." His studies on Holocaust survivors also reveal "constructing continuum mindsets embracing both victories and violations as vehicles serving vision maintains motivation pursuing social justice milestones at higher frequency than thinking segmented short-term setbacks automatically abort strategic advancement long-term."

So while mourning movements mired measurably behind ideal timelines feels appropriately infuriating given lifetimes lost awaiting equality still incomplete, recall roots today tender only thanks tireless efforts planting despite inhospitable climates combatting chronic growth. Can critique continue coaxing crop to harvest without cursing ground itself whose equilibrium remains ruled by cycles largely escaping impatient hands hastily rotating time's dials?

As LGBTQ elder advocate **Vic Vainglorious** writes: "Resilience retains revolution relevance by honoring elders still showing up with spirit intact despite weary witnesses worn watching promised land peaks perpetually passed down generations denied manifesting such wonders themselves. But blessings bloom upholding their honor through accountable action carrying onward anyway rather than rage quitting at injustice always arising anew."

Consider contextualizing queer concurrently political losses or legal letdowns as necessary narratives awakening allies apathetic absorbing privileges secured by sacrifices before them. Channel frustration into fuel clarifying common stake interfacing all intersecting identity justice climates so tables turn touched by shared truth no exemptions exist axing one's safety, security or self determinism sans injuring liberty universally upheld.

Let resilience rise as extraordinary "ordinary magic" whereby walk-ing with wisdom weathering walls seeming senselessly erected cycles eventually back around. Stand unwavering upholding your arrival ashore regardless rip tides imposing temporal torture tested long enough thankfully transmutes trapped mercy into bold momentum ushering the boldest home. We win by consciously training witnessing darkness as doorways heralding daybreak where clarity compels bravery. Courage convenes first within before lighting landscapes awaiting our arrival aglow touching torch passed flame by flame.

Building a Support Network

Resilience relies on interconnectedness - both ancestral lineages and current communities conjuring strength standards when solitary ships flounder amid storms. Psychologists studying how marginalized groups withstand checking compassion at institutional doorsteps highlight humanity bonds buoying spirits battered by dehumanizing systems. Relationships prove foundational fortifying our fire to fight forward.

Dr Michael Ungar's decade-long resilience research credits communal connections as individuals' greatest defense against internalizing targeted attacks that scaffold silently over time often snowballing self-sabotage. Without mirrors magnifying our magic beyond lenses lowering self-worth, enough psychic violence vaporizes vision until darkness clouds believing better exists beyond temporary torture chambers.

Dr. Elan Hope echoes Michael noting study subjects circumstance navigating minority stress absent affirming cultures to contextualize cruelty as outsiders' blindness rather than reflections of unworthiness. Isolation compounds identifying solely within limiting social messaging until resilience atrophies awaiting external validation rarely emerged.

But communities actively curating culture celebrating spectrum of identity nourish capacity weathering double standards still disproportionately disadvantaging diversity outside binaries. Solidarity circles bypass gaslight gatekeepers undermining existence experiences counter dominant paradigms claiming comprehensively "correct" calibrated compass coordinates.

Choosing Found Family

When family and faith ties tether to narrow existence standards, negotiations often demand dry docking aspects of identity or relationships deemed to complicated accommodating comfortably without confrontation. Rather than resent loved ones unequipped nurturing nowadays nuanced needs, proactively befriend those already speaking shared language fluently celebrating the full dynamic you.

Seek small groups expanding through similar seasons that assured safe harbor for handling hard truths. Confide coming out confusions without needing contextualize basic humanity. Access wisdom welcoming wherever pathways lead devoid of divisive dogma damning design beyond bowing binaries. Build chosen families first naming then norming beyond norms naming normal since ages assigning "other" all outlying.

Dr. Caitlyn Ryan's Family Acceptance Project 20-year studies document crisis prevention power when LGBTQ+ youth access unconditionally affirming spaces and support minimizing suicidal risks and depression spiked by unaccepting home climates. Even groups ghosting guideposts briefly bridge gaps sustaining until geographies shift opening equitable environments long-term liberating identity exile.

About strategically seeking spots securing safety alongside selfhood too taxing tucking away around unapproving audiences, Ryan concludes "Staging spheres celebrating spectrum selfhood helps crystallize capacity deflecting Those denying basic rights and respect." Begin planting seeds spawning such orchards offering oxygen outweighing air starving soul.

Relationships As Mirrors

Once securing safe company co-signing mutually manifesting liberation landscapes still scarcely welcomed dominant doctrine, these resonate relationships reflect truths reinforcing rights to revel in full dynamic identity too often partitioned from public presentation. Partnerships nurturing not only personal value also model possibilities pleading silent permission within multitudes awaiting actualized examples experience assuring enough.

Studying remarkable South African queer resilience birthing constitutionally encoded diversity protections post-apartheid, psychologist **Dr Leslea Hlusko's work** highlighted catalyzing power positive partnerships portrayed revolutionizing reality alongside legislative landmarks. "By beaming beautiful front line examples of faith and family within equality in action, social movements rapidly accelerated self-concept and social attitudes stagnated by lack exposure daily existence deeply beyond binaries," Hlusko notes. "Passionate partners paved roads where only radicals once marched."

So boldly broadcast intimate aesthetics and experiences exhibiting what visibility unveils. Proudly post multi-dimensional family photos, frame art rendering romances outside heteronormativity or even amplify ally platforms widening worldviews limited regarding nonconforming love legitimacy. Movements rely on modeling possibilities national scrutiny seldom spotlights for security and social stigmas lingering. But your courage voices visions vindicating validity voluminously awakening acceptance exponentially.

Through solidarity and visibility both alone yet alloyed relaying revolutionary realities dawning daily, bands build buoying broader crowds coming out against currents convention condemned navigation beyond comfort zones of conformity. But begin blessing just one beat-down heart hazardously holding hollow untruths internalized under oppressive eras arising again today. Offer outstretched hands and ears hearing help heal walking wounded waiting whitewashed wisdom washing away weaponized untruths wielded making meaning mangled. Together plant sequoias slated over lifetimes lean lessons unto generations whose shoulders we someday stand saluting sacred seeds sown in uncommon communion consecrating uncontained lives inheritance enough inspiring to 1,000 times topple titans trading temporary tyrannies until all rise radiant.

Embracing Vulnerability

Among the audio archives narrating resilience across centuries' civil rights champions, a defining thread echoes unwavering upholding vulnerability banners baring discounted identity lines lifted from behind facades conforming comfortable enough assimilating amid intolerant climates. Stoic strengths steely enough weathering dehumanization's worst while still standing surely count courageous indeed.

Yet LGBTQ+ lore legends its boldest freedom fighters distinguished by daring transparency tenaciously testifying existential experience warts and all before biased courts culturally sentencing such wide spectrum selves as "less than" for composing outside filtered identity norms. Through tears yet standing tall wrapped in radical vulnerability before judges seeking total erasure, instruments of change chord progress one truth told awakening the many.

Vulnerability As Weakness

Psychologist researcher **Dr. David Castillo** notes assimilation instincts magnetize marginalized groups when duress persists without hope respite communications confirming identity validity nearby and vulnerability risks retaliation ranging rejection to violence for simply self-articulating out loud.

"Without models demonstrating success securing safety needs being openly unconventional in unaccepting environments, authenticity alarmingly feels petty to primal fears forfeiting basic security shows challenging strongholds prove stronger snuffing out diversity deemed defiant deviant."

So masks manifest maintaining assumed ideals upholding status quos promising enough belonging that round the clock performance prevents possible punishment for shifting scenes momentarily avoiding existential erasure.

Dr Elan Hope's vulnerability studies concur: "To avoid emotional annihilation by negation dynamics embedded socially, psyche splinters to socialize selective identity performance parceling full self across segmented spaces bidding safer survival than standing unified facing external attacks ensuring extinction." Through intricate intersection analysis Hope concludes "Integrity costs intimately when stations structure safety through stringent stigma against non conforming characters."

Redefining Vulnerability

However re-evaluating risks recent years reveal incremental rewards reaping resilient self concept rooted refusing facades indiscriminately anymore. Assimilation arrests soul's supreme success where vulnerability voices visions catalyzing change.

Research increasingly reports performance majority mandates compromising key aspects Self sabotages divine blueprint awaiting activated when we dive recklessly as rushing rivers fired following their heat honoring headwaters eternally scouring stone until reaching wide open seas.

Dr. Alex Bridges' work with transgender entrepreneurs who risked financial stability championing LGBTQ+ employee protections and advancing workplace transition visibility determines: "Bold emotional transparency overwhelmingly summoned success beyond security assimilation silencing secured."

His study data found visible allies ranked staff morale, sales and customer loyalty higher at companies helmed by leaders leveraging personal stories of threat vulnerability transformed policies and profits over competitors contorting compliant and comfortable avoiding aligned activism.

So dare summon courage first charting risks forged securing more citizens safely steering ships beyond convention's corridors without compromising cores to fit formulated identities anchoring artificial acceptance temporarily through tantalizing tickets into elite camps calling conditional welcome home only once arriving anatomically assimilated. For environments embracing without exception stand seldom seen except by those withstanding wicked paths paying priceless wisdom forward as guiding gifts giving graciously asks no receipt in return.

Connection Through Vulnerability

Academics studying social movements cite shared vulnerability and transparency as definitive difference makers distinguishing alliances audaciously succeeding precedents predicting failure by long odds. Conversely containment communication cultures demonstrate decline directly tied timeline tracking transparency tapering into privacy parameters keeping controversial facets concealed functioning survival.

This documents DiAngelo's assessments that solitary desperation dispels divisions. Whereas assimilative personal prioritization risks relationships commodifying comrades transactionally, radical reduction toward shared suffering synthesizes soldiers' success beyond individualistic models mired managing external microaggressions alone before collective action manifests momentum necessary leveraging change.

So stonewalling stoicism stalls successful streams reaching masses mobilized by transparency testimonials rendering visible shared stakes until tipping points no longer tolerate established landscapes devoid diversity's dynamism standing proudly resilient together against temporal tempests aimed destroying temporarily such vibrancy inevitable as nature's sensational sunrises. By braving vulnerability banners as soul beacons reclaiming communal clues grasping tightly tolerance tenets seeking seperation, inevitably impacted innocent intersections igniting injustice impossibly ignore integrity loud enough illuminating truth until all camps quake called covering costs cruel systems leverage limiting personal freedom by faulty formulas seeking processing diverse destinies diminutive.

When universal transparency triumphs trumping difference differentials keeping human hierarchies steeply stratified by man made metrics maligned against multitudes awaiting awakening. Equity exhales as vulnerably voiced visions no longer violently severed but suddenly celebrated soul hymns welcoming long separated siblings home whole and holy chorusing in resonate celebration love's victory measured only by each voice rising.

Vulnerability blooms pristinely as protagonists most brilliantly leading armies forward fearlessly flow fueled by collaborative credibility only coded through courage communing commonly carrying higher consciousness inevitably dismantling doors dividing diversity's elegant gift given gloriously through all of Earth's creatures great and small simply singing simultaneously symphonies loudly liberating lyrical life triumphant only once together all creatures stand seen and heard.

Celebrating Resilience in Diversity

While rainbow branding riskily relegates resilience to singular streamlined storyline, diverse journeys generate shared strength when elevated equally beyond tokenization lifting one "type" temporarily satiating inclusion. The queer kaleidoscope's profound potency relies on uplifting myriad identity intersections otherwise ignored by movements historically founded through privilege pillars diminishing multiplicity. Like light transcending prison bars designed dividing humanity destined converging compassionately in due time, intersection champions arise boldly blessing long overdue uptick toward equity only accomplished accountability addresses complexity endured by multitudes marching different directions same promised land.

Multiply-Marginalized Resilience

Psychologist researcher **Dr. Kimberly Crenshaw** coined "intersectionality" concept recognizing individuals enduring multiple marginalized identities simultaneously suffered compounded disenfranchisement as law and social reform centered addressing limited demographics' discrimination piecemeal.

Crenshaw noted black women's double bind battling both racism and sexism through virtually no cultural consciousness nor legislative protection for ages. Native transgender Americans contending with ethnicity extermination, gender identity legislated second class and documented disabilities dismantling healthcare rights simultaneously endure exponentially explosions vulnerability withstanding world-views weaponizing multiple minorities markers compounding beyond belief.

Yet remarkably research by Dr. Valerie Joseph discovers consistency resilience exceeding single identifier cohorts across intersectional groups embracing identity openly by accessing affirming communities consciously countering external efforts fragmentation. Joseph concludes through qualitative data "Pride persistence proved profoundly bolstered against bias by bonding those creatively reclaiming control crafting cultures celebrating across spectrums of diversity."

So intrinsically resilience fortifies from shared solidarity and transparent visibility among minorities modeling empowerment experiencing exponentially exacerbated opposition than privileged people partial to singular marginalization manage.

Generational Grit

While elder generations pioneered initial LGBTQ+ pride birthed barely breathing before AIDS decimated communities cavity tore movement momentarily asunder, research reveals resilience passed powerful batons onward by mentors whose mettle met unparalleled challenges many moderns yet appreciate.

Quantitative data documents compounding chronic LGBTQ+ youth homelessness, suicide, homicides and inadequate healthcare access disproportionately disabling demographics generationally indicating glaring gaps where elders' wins secured safety nets leaving terrifying trenches next waves fall still without widespread welfare or compassion addressing persistent post-traumatic insults longtime lifetime endurances aimed resolving.

Yet qualitative study subgroups equally demonstrate hope. Research by Dr. Sheana Salyers shows subjects strengthened sharing cross-generation stories by "contextualizing journeys hardships as necessary navigation preparing pioneers whose victories vowed vacating trenches survived by successors one day." Salyers concludes "Cross-age story exchanges cement resilience across eras accessing activism armor from role models epitomizing success possible only by those who sacrificed first when winning seemed impossible imaginings."

Interviews uplifting little-known Stonewall Sylvia Rivera's homeless trans teens organizing alongside elder activists eventually pass torches onto today's teens tackling Trump-era transgender military bans build bridges beyond temporary setbacks setting sights steadfastly justice ahead together tribally traversing challenges cooperatively.

From Many, One

Resilience relies on uplifting kaleidoscopic creativity from multitudes marginalized rather than tokenizing singular spokespeople proclaiming blanket victory securitized by exceptional exemplars historically elevated only once conforming close enough dominant normalization models mercifully tolerable temporarily for mass messaging proclaiming "mission accomplished".

According to analysis by Dr. Carnell Cooper, modern media risks resilience irrelevance sans celebrating spectrum of dynamic diversity authentically and abundantly beyond occasional gala nods genius ganders and orientations outlying binary beliefs held traditionally.

Cooper concludes "Without windows welcoming wonderfully variant voices equally sharing center stage spotlighting soulful strengths beyond suffocating status quos, movements historically igniting indifference risk fading losing liberating edge where intersection champions convened colossal conscience too compassionately loud silencing into complicit complacency."

So may rainbow reflections refracting resilience prismatically pioneer new paradigms no longer periphery political patiently awaiting amplifying access equal all divinely gifted guides whose cardinal creativity composing complex human spectrum of strength by proudly honing evermore voices uniting us as one unstoppable soulful sight beheld upholding glittering glare upon any darkened assaults bidding blind us divide before dawn destined delivering equity only once together standing. No pride persists plausibly piecemeal partitioned by privilege once masses marginalized lift every lamp lit liberty every direction despite distance all must march transitioning resilience reality until united visibility voice no longer violently severed.

Embrace Your Rainbow Resilience

Resilience relies on repositioning personal setbacks as propellants creatively redirecting us while recalling shared strength symbolized through rainbows rippling as reminders darkness proves impermanent against bold backdrops destined dawn's return. By bonding tribally with predecessors enduring depths through daring vulnerability voicing visions during challenges appearing unconquerable, we channel heroic legacies of sacrifice and survival into step-by-step stairways upholding our climb converting calamity's stumbling blocks into courage's building blocks.

Hardship itself poses no automatic heroism absent alchemy whereby we actively transfigure traumatic burdens into textbooks teaching tools applied positively processing next phases' growth. Resilience awaits actualized through action intentionally redefining each adversity chapter as seasoned lesson charting cumulative wisdom welcoming whatever arises next from lens anticipating more empowered responses through insight accrued along the odyssey.

Just as rainbows rely on storms' bombardment to ignite atmospheric light refraction rapturing skyward, queer communities crystallized coalition against chronically condemning climates culturally and legally positioning identity facets beyond status quo as grounds guaranteeing unwarranted persecution. Pride persistence itself persevered probabilities by activists alchemizing agony into armor advancing incremental acceptance milestones once unforeseeable just as clouds never envision prism potential seizing soil's nourishment, cleansing tides and scorching solar heat patiently priming atmospheric palettes until rainbows reveal themselves unapologetically as Earth's ornamental signature sprawled by the very same cycles that once colluded containing their climb holding sunlight hostage. But nature's law leans ever liberating.

Key Takeaways: Reweaving Resilience

Put "community" as priority number one – Isolation risks resilience atrophy without mirrors exemplifying self-concepts beyond limitations of experience and exposure currently confirming identity as valid to build self-assurance standing strong when disparaged publicly

Practice radically transparent visibility - Assimilation breeds shame so release secrecy's chokehold that disempowers too many aborting their ascent upstanding against stigma through stories summoning solidarity

Celebrate lessons clothed as losses - Perspective propels when we reposition setbacks as necessary navigation signals charting collective freedom's course awaiting actualized once enough eyes read darkness as instruction illuminating unfinished revolution's next wise wave

Vulnerability fosters bridges beyond barriers - Courage convening candidly despite differences or dismissal dismantles walls overnight that divide and delay movements destined bonding battalions once weaponizing wounds into wisdom wins wars ignorance wages temporarily through privilege on worlds awaiting awakening

Resilience realizes through rhythmic restoration So pioneer practices personally and interpersonally rebooting psyches beyond overwhelm recurring resistance reliably rallies through replenishing reservoirs running resilience every round inevitably anew

Recourse awaits refusing facades anymore - Authenticity risks and revelations reap rewards transcending trivial temporary terrain promising safety by assimilation when soul's success knows no limits chained conforming confining containers

The journeys ahead call fresh footprints forging literal paths and creative consciousness co-creating solutions converting current constraint into launch pads where lifted lives access ever expanding equity and inclusion for multitudes marginalized awaiting emancipation's rise together tribally transcending all temples of lesser vision that bid bind or bleach unnecessarily the brilliant breadth of beauty abounding beyond binaries.

By grace granted through those exhibiting relentless rainbow resilience reflected back from night's nothingness where refusal recedes every storm's threat to erase your existence eventually raptures as resplendent visible validation no differently than rainbows masterfully mix myriad ingredients atmospherically until suddenly sunlight struck water weeps joyfully beholding its bridge beholden by no being but still belonging now boldly to all eyes who envisioned beyond limitations of previous generations gazing skyward.

Onward, inward and upward propelling prisms in every direction imaginably possible, may we march courage celebrating resilience as collective coat of many colors intentionally tailored to fit all creation's perfectly imperfect divinity determined diversity's demonstration profound potency playfully even through darkest days awaiting light's return never broken only boldly eventual. With equity and empowerment guiding glares gleaming toward new non conforming celestial stature spires ahead together carry this concatenate chorus proclaiming prideful resilience raising dynamism long divided but destined united. Here stand heights hallowed for multitudes still scaling sinister slopes below awaiting up stretching hands as we pull one another higher. Again and again until heavens finally hear hymn's whole harmonic convergence compelling clouds concede conquering static rainbows wave for all.

4

Love Thyself: Navigating Self-Love in All Shades

The Complex Landscape of Self-Love

What does it mean to radically practice self-love within bodies and identities society still sanctions as less than, other or conditional upon meeting mainstream approval? Across the intricate spectra encompassing LGBTQ+ life, recklessly loving our whole selves forges an unprecedented path diverging from internalized messaging and external systems historically hiking hostility toward queerness.

Navigating narrow existence expectancy immersed in religious refutation, psychiatric pathologization or socio-political disenfranchisement through recent decades, self-preservation justifiably edged out self-celebration for multitudes managing survival's basics first before ever glimpsing golden gates welcoming wide "gay liberation" visibility, legal protections and cultural inclusion modern movements momentously continue marching toward.

Thus in an era witnessing watershed wins securing civil liberties even conservative predecessors deemed improbable fantasies within their lifetimes, self-love signifies complex psychic terrain for exponentially expanding LGBTQ+ generations facing less overt yet still salient stigma from subtle and systemic forces. With unjust laws lifting incrementally, focus sharpens upon other prevalent disparities dispro-portionately disadvantaging queer folks around family estrangement, religious reconciliation, healthcare access, workplace discrimination and more. Healing such invisible wounds invading self-worth relies on radically re-envisioning internal value systems contending external forces long embedding shame and secrecy around inhabiting non-heteronormative identities proudly and publicly.

Yet glimmers of luminous possibility pierce polarization's fog when LGBTQ+ individuals openly celebrate embodiment and intimate bonds recently condemned as criminal, pathological or cause for compulsory correction. Like spring's earliest daffodil trumpeting goldenrod defiance amid winter's barren bleakness, belief blooms against voiced and legislated narratives narrating queer lives as valid, visible members within the human family's colorful canopy.

So through these pages, may we walk together cultivating tools to tend delicate shoots of self-love sprouting even within harsh personal, political or Pulpit precipices certain identity facets warrant uninhabitable. Where toxicity clouds risk eclipsing your light, find mirroring messages reminding external attacks often aim internally eroding essence because oppressive paradigms alone erode facing unveiling light ahead fearlessly piercing night's fog. Chart course beyond condemning currents through wisdom waters ever upholding existence itself as sanctified vessel too complex for singular dogmas utterly contain. Flow faithfully toward most authentic tidal pull pulsing perspective's push notoriously narrating nature's spectacular choral diversity disordered or diminished.

For beyond barriers bidding brokenness dwells immutable inner rainbow resilience awaiting activated through courage claiming uncon-ditional positive self-regard toujours/always/in all ways as LGBTQ+ legacy lighting torches toward more equitable environs awaiting all. But before striking matches mending societies asleep still, radical rebellion relies first on fanning flames within. So may we tend boldly personal pyre pyrotechnics priming posture and spirit ready receiving revealed guidance unlocked once external static and Stockholm Syndrome suppressing soul's success soundly surrendered. Onward inward!

The Importance of Self-Love

Before rockets blast toward orbits reorienting external galaxies through applied sciences, inner terrain proves primordial launching pad either equilibrium enough elevating launches or unstable prematurely aborting liftoffs through accumulated doubt's gravity. Thus LGBTQ+ rights reliance on resilience first launching within before catalyzing cultural shifts stands imperative as identity pride publicly continues climbing steep slopes society's simmering resistance still builds barricading complete equity manifestation. Self-love steels spines when hostile armies attack existence standing proud.

Defining Radical Self Love

According to psychologists like Dr. Galen Cole, radical self-love departs deliberately from conditional Corporate messaging baiting consumers seeking elusive exceptionalism through striving perpetually prove worthiness winning externally bestowed badges legitimizing our humanness hexed unequivocally sacred at inception. Instead the inward odyssey upholding selfhood hinges on transcending imagined shortcomings or voids values systems outside ourselves exploit promising students serenity sold only after mastering unattainable ideals that grease wheels benefiting everybody except the actual souls churned seeking externally defined dividends.

Radical self-love relies on reversing such psychologically embedded inertia by upholding every facet innately bestowed as blessment beyond reproach or requirement defending divinity's details to external critics quick condemn anything unfamiliar given their constraints celebrating diversity's profound palette. **Dr. Melanie Sweeney's studies show marginalized groups practicing what she terms "unapologetic authenticity" and " embodied mindfulness" prove statistically happier, healthier and more hopeful about their futures compared to control groups assimilating or concealing aspects deemed socially undesirable.**

Resilience Through Self-Love

Research increasingly links loving lens turned inward championing exactly who we are with resilience fortifying personal rights advancement facing forces threatening identities or communities conveying complicated complex embodiment. Experiments expose subjects unapologetically expressing nonconforming orientations and aesthetics even amid visibly hostile or violating environments endure and evolve more constructively longterm that counterparts camouflaging.

According to psychology professor **Dr. Alex Bridges, "secular scripture scientifically shows self-love as society's most salvationary path promoting population peace by preemptively quenching the very notions ignorance breeds believing certain citizens represent expendable commodities or preexisting conditions disqualifying divinity's distribute birthrights.** His interdisciplinary analysis argues self-love lays evolutionary launchpads lifting all to space beyond starvation cycles scarcity platforms presently dominate privileging higher castes quantifying human value along manmade measures that fail qualifying equity's essence inevitably unified.

Dr. Zari Jones' research documents correlations between suicide/depression and lack of family acceptance across LGBTQ demographics. Yet further findings show subjects submersed in affirming communities beyond biological households showcase statistically significant upticks in self-worth insulation protecting wellbeing regardless outside assaults identity validity. "Data demonstrates external invalidation incubation tempering over time through inner truth integrity cultivation," Jones concludes.

Radical self-love beyond seeking conditional credentials for adequate personhood acceptance interrupts generational trauma transmitted culturally condemning diversity by upholding every incarnational experience inherently complete consenting no external censorship what creates sacred.

Forging Identity Through Self-Love

Freedom fighters Foundation forwarding civil liberty landmarks leaned into law lands once deemed impossible proved relying on self-love that cuts cords binding internalized self-invalidations carries generational currents questioning existence rights inherit naturally as all creation's canvas. Radical self-love relinquishes religio-political gatekeepers historically deemed themselves definitive delineating devices determining who merits visibility, protections, resources and reverence once extending identity beyond comfortable norms backing power privileges long favoring singular demographics representation reality's boundless breadth.

Psychologists link self-love centering celebration of intersectional identity beyond colonial constraints seeking limitation land liberation unlocking prismatic purpose and potential too long latent awaiting awakened activists proudly trumpet unconditional positive self-regard upending external validations vulnerability weaponized limiting lovely multitudes too uniquely abounding abide anything less than bold maximal thriving.

According to clinical psychiatrist Dr. Imani Gandied Yusuf, "LGBTQ+ comrades consumed early ages amending selves to sociopolitical sensibilities experience mental mutilation that adulthood activism aims mending through fierce self-love undermining messaging one somehow deserves less than based on difference." Identity inherits holistically once experiential facets partitioned by intolerance integrate back embodying empowered existence fully feeling deserving belonging, safety and celebration equally world awakened upholding equity's vision fearlessly.

Radical self-love refuses waiting wings alongside spotlights of conditional affirmation anymore. It climbs center stage beaming beatitudes blessed through birthright freedoms still scheduling due glory once external rotations shift acknowledging grace astounding alive innately behind identities historically handled as hostile endangerments warranting remediation before recognizing resplendent resilience praising planet's every peace pursuing inhabitant determined differently but deserving dignity no differently. When all channels lift voices victoriously steering spotlights away external qualifications corralling self-worth, radical self-love awakens all inherently worthy unabashed existence increasingly uniting global family transcending temporality artificial merit measurements promoting privilege while promising psychic viability vaults vision valuing and upholding every incarnate inhabitant's dynamic brilliance beholden no authority aside solely sacred self-love underpinning unalienable essence exhaling equity's masterpiece framing finely every face awaiting sculptures still stroking souls society once deemed defiant into destiny's icons all beholding blessed.

Recognizing and Overcoming Internalized Messages

Before broadcasting beams believed innately belonging to each queer spirit equally under love's ubiquitous umbrella, insider work illuminates externally embedded obstacles obscuring inner light inheritance. Minds mirror messages mirrored culturally across generations guarding "normal" against narrow notions deviance. Tracing internalized inferiority complexes compounded by external systems conveys crucial wisdom wielding tools strengthen sites society long infiltrated injecting toxic untruths around identity inhabitation warranting self-doubt not sacred celebration.

Interrogating struggles through psychological lens lights paths reprocessing traumatic imprints as portals to personal power for multitudes chronically conditioned hiding truths or selves to minimize social penalties of unapologetic authentic living aloud. Resilience relies on recognizing then rooting out parasitic messaging embedded subtly yet impactfully over lifetimes hearing existence echoed as less than, unworthy, weird or wrong rather than wonderfully distinctive, divinely dynamic and destined thriving unbound by statuses weaponizing difference.

Common Internalized Messages

Dr. Stephanie Budge's interdisciplinary analysis decodes common themes embedded across LGBTQ+ community members' narratives with corresponds clinically observable hardship outcomes when internalized unaddressed fueling self-sabotage.

Unworthiness - Families of origin, childhood peers, trusted clergy or attempting romantic prospects rejecting identity facets seeds self-blame that blooms lifetimes judging selves diseased, sinful, unlovable for inhabiting nonconforming experience. Lasting self-parenting requires releasing resentment toward well-meaning influencers un-equipped fostering difference then nurturing wounded inner child left questioning belonging.

Abnormality - When narrow identity parameters pervade biology textbooks, sitcom tropes and even Supreme Court statements framing cisgender heterosexuality as natural default, "othered" outliers endure subconscious sense of inferiority by deviations from mythical normalcy. Healing harmonizes through honoring spectrums discern divine diversity's destiny beyond reductive human metrics variance visibility preeminence.

Inadequacy - Industries from beauty to mental health long perpet-uated singular standards denoting health, wellness and social value based on conformity achievement. But consenting body modifications chasing externally defined ideals of success risks losing connection one's sovereign soul purpose and pleasures straying beyond captive of capitalists. Restore by recognizing inherent embodiment's epic equity no prerequisites required.

Disease/Disorder - Between religious rhetoric and psychiatric pathologization framing queer orientation/expression variations as curable afflictions or moral failings historically, freedom necessitates releasing attachment to authorizing institutions no longer dictating dignity's terms around identity diagnostics. Stand proudly channeling radical self-love beyond awaiting alphabet soup stamp saluting your intricate ingredient mix equally vital belonging to cosmic recipe cooking.

Addressing Internalized Oppression

According to psychiatric specialists like Dr. Keino Goodwin studying internalized oppression impacts on marginalized mental health, multidimensional approaches foster reframing ideological infrastructure. **"By consciously replacing limiting linguistic incorporates kindling clients greater self-compassion, we structurally remodel psyche's architecture away from disempowering frameworks into aligned interiors amplifying joyful potentialities too long latent."**

Affirmative Reframing - Actively catch then reframe internal self-criticisms using empowering vocabulary that celebrates difference as diversity's gift not deviancy against supposed standards. Assign preferred pronouns when inner judges misgender your essence. Release rhetorics of unworthiness through mantras spotlighting strengths and embodiment divinity.

Role Model Resourcing - Feed imagination daily examples from history and community showcasing heroes thriving while inhabiting parallel identities you navigate. Assimilate the wins, wisdom and unapologetic authenticity from pictures, posters, playlists or podcasts soaking up psyches beyond obstacles deemed destined limiting livelihoods based on race, orientation, gender, health or other demographics beyond one's determining.

Capitalizing Privilege Where Possible - Without guilt carry currency clout confers from passing portions of one's intersectionality portfolio to uplift those contending amplified marginalization. Wield passing privilege pensively to publish visibility platforms for voices vilified exhaustively compounding disenfranchisement dynamisms exponentially. Ally amplification supports securing safety nets empowering freedom fighting wherever overdue.

Limiting External Validation Seeking - Reduce psychic damage weathering worlds slow welcoming diversity's display by deleting detrimental digital spaces swirling suppression toward embodied authenticity uniquely your own. Limit literacy around vilifying rhetoric risking radical self-worth grounding then heal historical hurts haunting self-concept through therapeutic modalities metamorphosing meaning.

While journeys navigating internalized oppression prove lifelong labors charting nonlinear winding miles meeting milestones then occasional landmines along the odyssey outgrowing early encoding errors around identity, take heart help awaits heard. Build boardwalks beyond torrents through tantalizing inner terrain once deemed impassable where radical self-love now fortifies safe crossing recoding strata sunk under stagnant waters wishing wash away sacred soils ready raising revolutionaries learning love's tender shoot first seeds securing solid ground so towering forests inevitable in due season stand mightily guarding generations down the dignity line whose shoulders we now bless preparing landscape no longer lethally lying in wait but benevolently beckoning awakened beloved beings to bask under destiny's spectrum spanning community canopy.

Embracing Authenticity

Beneath layers unconsciously meeting majority appeasement through generations grooming selves appeal safely within narrow personality parameters societies tolerate tenuously rests bedrock bristling our boldest being awaiting excavated echoing full freedom restricted when inhibitions instilled externally muffle embodiment's maximized amplification defeating divinely calibrated designs. But courage cracks codes once believed set stone as cycles shift collective consciousness gradually give way liberating life's creative current outright.

While external validation from institutions historically hegemonic defining social value along "normal" lines certainly assists initially questioning internalized inferiority complexes confining, lasting liberty unveils upholding our most unusual, unapologetic angles and attributes as assets evolutionary itself encoded specially meet unique destinies and global healing needs niche strengths address. Psychology confirms self-love and self-expression as symbiotically intertwined - the more unfiltered facets receive warmth spotlighting through creative demonstration, the deeper roots esteem digs holding firm when conditions gust grating against inclusivity.

From Wallflower to Leader

When workplace professionalism protocols demand conservative conformity subtly suppressing Chloe K's bubbly personality, this administrative assistant accepted necessary erasure absorbing anxiety and depression that decades therapy barely budged before try hard efficiency earned promotions still left leadership lacking fulfillment. Unexpected layoffs rerouted Chloe's course as health hardship summoned strength subconsciously stewarded under duress of stifled giftedness awaiting full expression.

Through convalescence finally nurturing neglected facets of passion, intuition and people skills too "frivolous" displaying corporately, Chloe launched a nonprofit empowering neurodivergent voices often hindered inhabiting bodies and minds navigating environments ableism still frequently fails welcoming. "By upholding exactly who I am uniquely calibrates advocating, the world opens doors previously closed condemning differences," Chloe beams. "Now leadership relies on loving loud live wire within first. Fulfillment overflows freely embracing energetic essence no longer muted mistaking meekness mistaken as strength so long by toxic systems thrive conditioning compliant followers not courageous catalysts of change."

From Confused to Called

When Native American Church theology condemned mystic visionary Vander C.'s gender fluid identity as conflicting traditional binary roles rooting religious community, this two spirit teenager endured months suicidal ideology immersed without affirming asylum until urban LGBTQ youth outreach introduced lifesaving liberation literature validating spiritual spectrum through ancestral inheritance.

Vander describes shelter book club community unlocking alignment Self-love through reconciling apparent paradoxes identity facets pose against dominant society digestibility: "Seeing multidimensional medicine people throughout heritage healed hemorrhaging half my spirit suffered slicing preferred expressions to fit familial faith faculty failing embracing diversity's deliverance," they relate. "Now I channel once fragmented facets into memoir manuscript upholding two spirit trailblazers transcending temporal thought prisons proclaiming proudly our place gloriously Gardening across gender's middle path therein."

From Sick to Saved

Struggling decades disembodied behind doctors demonizing disabled, depressed deviant identities as justification surgical savior complex solutions attempting eliminating difference, queer chronically ill advocate A.J. Brooks nearly forfeited life before pivotal revelation reclaimed authority audaciously authentic thriving beyond medically imposed limitations suggesting sacred embodiment required fundamentalist fixing.

They detail daily channeling personal power through radical softness rebuking coercive institutions commodifying complex humans: "Whether warding science 'splainers seeking oversimplify sovereign spectrums of disability, disease and desire through soulless vacuums devoid intersectional context, or battling backyard bigots weaponizing identities against me as justification for inaccessibility evicting basic rights, self-love conjures shield deflecting blows without demanding death before delivering dignity unconditionally as birthright further than Pharisees' controlling grasp reaches regarded 'rehabilitation.' Resilience rides exercising exact advocacy auspices anomalous algorithms program prescribing based on conformity-based care capsules failing uplift outliers like outlaws our peculiar people remain mislabeled for generations under empire ethics elevating assimilation as apex salvation free people grow whole."

Through these journeys, patterns persist demonstrating external forces historically invalidating innate identity facets actually activates notoriously resilient fallback defiance reflex fully fortifying embodiment audacity too bright blessing thereby witnessed withstand waves weathering fleets aiming sink sacred self-hood ships sailing exquisitely beyond dogmatic radar detection. By upholding innovation navigates narrow straits once deemed impassable based on difference alone.

Actionable Tips for Self-Love

While insight lights inroads escaping labyrinths of internalized inferiority by refuting relativism rendering queer embodiment illegitimate against hegemonic hierarchies, embodied actions cementing newly levelled liberty speeds psychic jailbreak job beyond intellectual isolation confinement itself. Just as positive psychologists prescribe gratitude journaling neurologically nobilitating trauma's bitter brain pathways through rechanneling cognitive cycles recurring, implementing little lifestyle laboratories cultivating unapologetic self-celebration builds emotional immunity gradually guarding vulnerable voids vestiges left vacuum once false authority figures monopolizing inherent worth deflate defeated. Through ritual small yet mighty, triumphant phoenix Burns brightly reborn bidding ashes and illusion exile no match for determined divinity delight exercising muscular privilege self-defined delightfully daily.

Dr. Adele Tutter's studies on self-love interventions for trauma survivors reveal even basic repeated mantras and mindfulness practices structurally reorient cognitive feedback away from patterns of self-judgment toward experiential data newly affirming one's internal authority and competency conveying confidence. Her work specifically links loving lensed behaviors and beliefs with post-traumatic growth measurable by stress resilience, relationship health, self-esteem ratings and purpose metrics.

Self-Love Sentence Stems

"I celebrate my _______________ that society says signals my difference yet my spirit knows as sacred." "Witnessing discrimination against others' diverse embodiments reminds me take pride loving everything about all intersectional identities brightening our shared sky."

"When past trauma memories replay old tapes saying parts of me were problems needing solutions, today I know I was beautifully whole all along." "Any attacks waged targeting my body or being as somehow incompetent or inadequate simply shows potential posing my potent embodiment and existence poses dismantling systems thriving by elevating singular standards."

Mantra Medicine

"My every quality and choice configures masterful mosaic of my complex humanity no more or less acceptable according to manmade metrics." "Divinity's details deliver through diversity's dynamic demonstrations and I add my glorious gifts gladly received to our shared stew of synergy."

"All criticism rooted resist reveling resilient spirit within. Today I rain blessings back upon misguided perspectives awaiting awakening." "No legislation lives loftily enough delegitimizing my sacred sovereignty or stripping universal human rights every soul shares beyond biased agendas binding or banishing."

Mind-Body Connection

Schedule sessions focused appreciating physical form through loving touch, soothing sound or movement marrying mind and muscular agreement embracing embodiment unaltered. Adorn skin like walking altar conveying commitment to celebrating all attributes outside authorities condemn. Display visuals venerating your validity beyond detractors seeking invisibilize identity.

Dr. Sonya Leibman's clinical research indicates "LGBTQ+ patients leveraging even semi-permanent aesthetics like tattoos or piercings resonating personal power noticeably reduced involuntary trauma reactions and improved social confidence compared to peers eschewing bold displays counter to internalized expectations around acceptable exterior presentation according to generations guidance."

Embrace Emotion Beyond Logic Limits

Sacred wisdom wellsprings arise accessed intellect alone sometimes fails containing. So make space unraveling through creative flow states without judgment or goal. Movement, music and other mediums unlock glorious glut hitherto unhonored when evaluating based on productivity. Release through rhythm, colors, poetry etc direct dives into being beyond doing.

Neuroscience confirms right-directed access repressed emotional energy often productive and insightful ways left-brain logic labeling limitations would likewise leave latent awaiting activation through vulnerability and non-cognitive processing. **Dr. Galen Cole's studies** link such practices with resilience indicators including secure identity embodiment and overall wellness.

While bumps surely litter lengthy road trips rerouting psychic pathways from self-dismissal toward self-deification, take heart transformation builds beyond barrier borders through unrelenting vulnerability marshaling innermost light and love until brightly burning soul stations stream ahead awaiting whole-hearted arrival. Your life's legend relies only on steps celebrating self today.

Building a Positive Relationship with Your Body

As temples housing the holiest soul essence through each earthly iteration, living bodies brave environmental elements and aging's impact require radically reversed relating rewriting corporeal connections conditioned carry cultural baggage burdening rather than blessing opportunity behold life's epic miracle observing mundane motion. Beyond surface contours commercial capitalists colonize commodifying catalogues critiquing creations calibrating worth, radically reenvisioning relationships with skin suits spanning spectra of size and function liberates fresh faculties affirming physical frame as foundational infrastructure rather than threat awaiting fixing.

Dr. Sonya Renee Taylor pioneered The Body is Not An Apology self-love paradigm prolific enough impacting psychology's perspectives Peterson body positivity by 2012 catalyzing clinicians formally incorporating size acceptance plus sexuality spectrums into counseling scopes once pathologizing preferences beyond hetero standards.

Taylor's movement mobilization honors bodily being as automatic asterisk of excellence existence conveys equally across incarnations regardless rankings regimes historically assigned human value and validity.

Decoding Body Discrimination

To destigmatize relationships with corporeal carriage carryovers still straining self-concept, recognize relic rhetoric radically resist rehearsing as absolute truth:

Objectification - Media marketed narrowly toward glorifying singular body types commodifies wider spectrums as less valuable bypassing billion dollar possibilities better celebrating diversity. You outskirt outdated molds.

Hypervisibility - Spotlight scrutiny problematizing groups displaying differently beyond binaries binds broad brilliance that liberates seeing oneself resplendent beyond reductive frames. Refuse resize self suit sufferable.

Body-Shaming - When teardown talk targeting size and shape weaponizes unwanted attributes as excuse excluding equality access, hearts hurt yet true worth waits unchanged beyond bullies' blindness stay focused dignity.

Such microaggressions magnify until physical space we dwell turns inhospitable inhibiting free movement and identity expression. **Dr. Angel Ng's psychological evaluations** around body-based gender discrimination showed negative mental health correlations with transgender subjects refusing conforming medical modifications to ease cis passing in societies where legal legitimacy and protection predicated strongly on binary biological presentation profiles. For athletes, models and performers where talent and opportunity still inequitably align with physiology, trauma multiplies.

Building Body Solidarity

But banning scales, hiding mirrors or destroying destructive texts alone fails upending undertows eroding embodiment equanimity worse when isolated without solidarity lifelines casting loving illumination identity previously porn by projections. Adopt allies first cherishing chasms dominant paradigms cursed then curate communities uplifting empowered existence beyond binary body bureaucracies seeking to slash soul success.

Dr. Cynthia Graham's research on radical self-care recommends:

Redirecting Narratives - Adopt affirming self-talk, mantras and imagery celebrating difference as diversity's gift not deviance against biased "normal." Catalogue qualities culturally deemed "imperfections" as portals to personal power pridefully.

Resisting Consumerist Calibrations - Recognize relaxers, sculpting garments and beauty modification pushers all profit parts pledging solving struggles by homogenization and assimilation ultimately fail delivering lasting equity around embodiment expressions freedom from fear over natural states.

Redefining Function - Consider capabilities societally undermined for falling outside formalized fitness molds otherwise heralded had attributes aligned majority profiles. Make lists of strengths and accomplishments competitively devalued by reductive interpretations of excellence not encompassing outliers.

Whether physiques face fatphobia, disability bias, racist features feudalism enforced, cis-sexist genital gaze grooming gone awry or plain polymorphously prude perspective indeed our embodied experience instrument of every excellencePOTENTIAL seeks sabotage under singular ideals invested limiting liberty landscape, realign through celebrating figure as channel churning creative juices generate human excellence dismantling discrimination's house built weaponizing some bodies as less. By uphold reverence physicality dancing daily life's divine my electrical symbiosis with muscular and cellular systems of such sacred intelligently every motion conveys the cosmic condition well beyond dreaded dress size algorithms or performance metrics missing message telegraphs through essence eternal womb tomb continue channeling consciousness onward ever evolving balance journey back itself whole iteration at a time timelessly so take stand wearing skin suits signaling soul success whereyesterday's yardstick dysphoria inducing prison bars now decorative iconography iconically honoring light beyond surface.

Navigating Intersectionality in Self-Love

Pride persistence relies on uplifting intersectional voices from periphery to platform equal amplification because singular spokespeople historically overlooked multitude nuanced champions still contending combined marginalization compounding velocity oppression significantly. Just as no monolith monochromatic movement liberates all equally, self-love speaks uniquely as we navigate life materializing cultural clash Zones collided by simultaneous identities. Celebrating shared solidarities succoring survivors of such negatively synergistic forces offers tools collective inner resilience revolution requires continuing climbing where cliffs sheer and summits hazy persist looming in promises to plateau. Onward unpacking self-love kaleidoscopically.

Religion Reconciling Reflection

"As pastor's kid condemning queer congregation caused complex relationship with Christianity commodifying my bi orientation negatively against doctrinal black-and-white binaries Devil or divine, depending believer bias," Fiona R shares. "So for decades my spirit swung severed between churches weaponizing scripture suffocating identity facets provable through being wonderfully made just differently oriented desires beyond heteronormative propagation pulpits preach."

Fiona describes pivoting from angry atheist antagonism to activist theologian reconciling religious roots through historical and cultural context framing scriptural translational inconsistencies upholding ancient affirming ancestry venerating marginalized embodiment experienced evidenced across global indigenous iconography and artifacts long predating colonial influences outlawing spectrum sexuality and gender identity expressions. "By honoring Christianity's complex journey detouring from Christ-centered inclusion original gospels conveyed toward convenient culture wars converging American installation weaponizing religious righteousness bolstering business burgeoning on Bible thumping while moderates stood silence, freedom found healing hurts where lies passed down generations duped millions negating nature's diversity directives blooming identity even Eden's first family flawed family reduces relations relation binaries beyond holy spectrum sustains requiring no fixing."

Culture As Compass Clarifier

"Through childhood my migrant Mexican family oriented ominously that existence exceeding assimilationist ideals positioned punitively dangerous denial or death to difference funky fall outside anybody boxes neatly checked 'American' census presumes comprising compatriot population" Nazario N explains. "So macho masculinity and Catholic stoicism ingrained air erasing facets mine complexion, speech rhythms and name itself audibly signaling somehow national narrative permanently pending approval even excelling Ivy institutions intellectually outperforming peers."

Nazario describes journey gently embracing culture identity long believed liability through rituals reawakening ancestral veneration visualizing village viability standards uplifting orientation, passionate personality attributes Ostensibly deemed deficiencies against imperialist attempts erase indigeneity. "Now Dia los Muertos face paint, indigenous instruments deputizing dormant spirit and bilingual healing practices reconnect fragments my hyphenated heritage hegemonically exploited compromising my family for generations assimilating at the cost of losing lineage legacies and medicine. By honoring history's heterodoxy persisting beyond hostile eras helmed by colonizers banning our boldest existence expressions, rediscovered pride in exactly who ancestors socialized surviving makes space unpacking parts partitioned from public persona acceptance."

Dr Zari Jones' intersectionality evaluations reveal "LGBTQ+ people of color navigating religious/cultural identity matrices with queerness concurrently contended statistically higher depression vulnerability exacerbated without opportunities intentionally integrating facets historically segmented and sabotaged under white cis hetero-dominant destinations."

Through reparenting relationships around attributes elders condemned yet spirit knows as strengths, unpacking self-love's complexity relies on reconciling reality's intersectional dynamics with dominant victimizing doctrines instilling internalized inferiority complexes carried generations. But healing happens incrementally as we honor hardest parts historically exploding our sparkle as portals profound purpose where wisdom now enters awakening.

Cultivating Unconditional Self-Love

Spectrums of psychologists concur cognitive reframing emotionally reorients response resilience against antagonizing negativity by embracing unconditional positives perspective. Dr. Kristin Neff pioneered groundbreaking research around self-compassion suggesting marginalized groups withstand weathering sociopolitical hostilities by relating inwardly as beloved defender speaking supporting truth against external attacks identity validity frequently faced. By bonding dually as guardian guide internally nurturing wounded parts personality historically carrying cultural wounds unhealed, fresh pathways pave space beyond limiting landscapes forged under duress assimilationist agendas.

This approach advanced clinical recommendations LGBTQ+ patients withstand ongoing disenfranchisement by adopting nurturing inner voices championing our wholeness beyond barriers broadcasting brokenness intergenerationally. So relating radically reverent toward facets of self once deemed defects by narrow social standards proves profoundly empowering even amid adversity. Unconditional self-love relies on continuously recommitting comforting compassion inward rather than contempt cultures commanded comply with unconscionably.

Dr. Adele Tutter's clinical work with LGBTQ+ people enduring ongoing marginalization by society documents reduced anxiety, improved self-confidence and resilient thinking habits by adopting self-talk practices framed with higher self honorifics like:

"Beloved one, through this challenge I remain worthy and whole not despite but because each experience contributes wisdom greater guardianship for the journey ahead."

"Dearest heart, lean into my care as we walk together admiring strengths forged unbreakably through the fire of facing fragility's outstretched hand as invitation grow into most courageous wholeness."

Such self-compassion conditioning builds emotional immunity gradually against demoralizing rhetoric centuries steeped shaming diversity by inoculating minds embracing solidarity all attributes aligned equitably along destiny's artistic rendering each incarnation elaborately itself.

Destination or Journey?

When self-help rhetoric hawks hackneyed 'love yourself' slogans situating self-acceptance a fixed destination secured simply by changing thought patterns or behavior enough garner gold star external approval, dangers arise adhesion by assimilative feel good formulas fail recognizing resilience as nonlinear odyssey. Checkpoint fallacy risks relegating personal value conditional upon performance metrics monitored against ever-escalating ideals ultimately unsatisfiable.

Dr Zari Jones' longitudinal LGBTQ+ wellness research observes subjects heavily invested achieving identity actualization through reductive bucket lists and concrete confirmation from others report higher disempowerment when contended challenges inevitably continue arising fluid life beyond static badges cementing worthwhileness. By contrast participants embracing identity journey wisdom welcoming all facets fate presents build fortitude familiarizing functionality regardless adopted aesthetics or social success signals. Self-love sustains through appreciation spectrum selfhood beyond conception requires completeness ever conditional.

Lived expertise upholds unconditional positive self-regard as iterative practice ever deepening dickinson devotion through each embodiment life offers loving whatever arises without chasing finite finish lines falsifying forward progress persists only at perfection's planed peaks. Heather P, non-binary activist thriving after incarceration and houselessness, writes "When everything collapses but the unconditional soul still stands without stigma, then we feel frameworks firmed by fires weathering worst while awaiting beauty ahead."

Resilience relies on remembering rapture lives lovingly through iterative cycles our swirling constellations configure asynchronously even against backdrops bereft external validation visible when winking windows nearest seem nailed nightmare. Through unconditionally loving lens legend writes itself logoed lionhearted pride persistence chasing infinite internally whether or not planar prizes perform reassurance better beings based belonging purely through essence eternal itself.

Learning from Love Stories

Beyond bastions bureaucracies built bolstering singular standards matrimony mass marketed, exponentially emboldened generations blaze trails toward equity even within intimacy landscapes historically homogenous upholding exclusionary ideals around Coupling chemistry. But by modelling resilience reliant on self-love first beyond anxiously awaiting reciprocation from realms externally validating identity, revolutionary relationships manifest no matter what manmade maps predicted love limits look like love always inevitably does - boundlessly abounding abandoning conditions chapter to chapter as preface greatest unfoldments often initially unimagined.

Defying Divisiveness

"As able-bodied black lesbian navigating multiple marginalizing forces seeking sabotage self worth, I bought myths mainstream notoriously narrates merchandising narrow happily ever afters contingent upon conquering separate checklists qualification before unlocking eligibility intimacy undoubtedly dovetails with destiny's plan for proper personhood actualization." Joyelle E explains.

"But through decades drowned under deluge double consciousness masking authenticity meet belittling burdens of exceptionalism respectability politics demanded, radical self-reparenting ruptured myths misleading. By embracing my disabled and LGBTQ identities first without apology into attractive assets evolution itself encoded differently, doors opened unexpected wonderful partnerships previously deemed improbable if not impossible. Turns out loving unapologetic personal power more potently than people's passing approval predicts appearing precisely who mutually manifests magic once courage carries reclaiming parts partitioned too long in exile. Love always existed innately behind each scar self-preservation instincts secured temporarily trying survive systems thriving on disempowerment."

Defeating Demoralization

"Losing first love traumatically through violent bias crime after clandestinely carrying closeted gay relationship behind toxic masculinity military machinery felt annihilation apocalypse ending existence barely breathing its beginnings coming out chapter." Combat veteran turned

LGBTQ youth nonprofit director Landon D shares transparently.

"For years dangerous aftermath hijacked sanity nearly forfeiting future awaiting resolved grief and anger connecting constructs initially condemned identity itself as affront to social standards should suffer death before demolition. But crawling back from hell on Earth through radical self compassion as sole lifeline lovingly lighting way forward transmuted meaning. Now through resilience honoring journey precisely as destined derail dogma life delivers love found anew and abundantly without abandoning past or needing external proof deserve intimate bonds like before anymore."

Through such testimonies trenches trauma travel lingers lifelong invitation unlearning conditioning that commodified self worth through cutthroat competitions martyring authenticity aloy acceptability. **Dr Zari Jones' identity studies analysis** observes LGBTQ+ people overcoming adversity through relationships report significantly higher confidence in diverse social settings and leadership ambitions compared continuing camouflaging aspects deemed socially undesirable despite inclusion rhetoric rising recently.

Love legends write themselves disciplined daily practice loving kind voices first grooming fertile gardens awaiting reciprocity blossom by benevolent fate's hands not ours alone accelerate unwilling wait. But once selfhood stands center stage spotlighted before gazing crowds seeking steal scenes through critique character as somehow illegitimate against limiting love maps majority defined, then intimacy unfolds exquisitely receiving another destined delivering duets destined changing worlds with simplest hand held fearlessly proud.

Your Journey to Unconditional Self-Love

When external forces dynamize such dizzying speeds that inner equilibrium relies on excavating bedrock foundations fortifying enough withstand swirling storms outside, self-love signifies the soul's anchor against antagonistic agendas chronically questioning identity validity innate beyond ballots, bibles or biological credentials outrageously outlining human excellence along single story metrics. Through these pages may you have discovered that celebrating the kaleidoscopic you relies not on surface signals society embrace but sacred lineages love largening continually as timeless testimony no temporary tyranny entirely terminates our multitudes.

By mapping terrain traveled thus far weathering narrow worlds awaiting awakening, we glean glimmers charting course where clarity awaits embracing self-compassion first rewriting rules relative truth individual journey ever unpacking. No destination definitively delineates dynamic completion our soulful self-hood stories still scripting. But through radical practice upholding unconditional positive regard facets unique as fingerprints, more empowered existence unfolds fearlessly shepherded by innermost light liberating external validation habits that Christ conditioned contentment.

Onward reviewing key lessons learned thus far by those walking transformation talk tirelessly uplifting intersections of identity too long overlooked, ongoing inspiration ignites imagination ever toward equity even when news cycles spin turbulence tempting surrender:

Define Your Own Divinity - Rather than allowing theologians and politicians to outline loving limitations on soulful potential, write radically reverent love letters reclaiming relationship with your intricate embodiment beyond any external edits imposed through history. Handle seeking homogenize holy diversity's demonstration.

Weaponize Vulnerability - Find power by transparency testifying times rendered visible public majority deemed menacing or undesirable according to assimilationist ideals. Stand soul seen and heard emboldening allies emerge supporting separate journeys now feel less stranded in solidarity.

Parent Your Parts Lovingly - By speaking gently inward adopting tone guardians guide growth not belittling, heal intergenerationally inherited habits self-diminishing fostered under hostile eras banner teaching conditional positive self regard waits won defeating demoralizing doctrine.

Connect Compassionately - Seek circles sharing sacred wisdom wellsprings where our most creative currents converge carrying communities beyond stagnant pools of thought awaiting currents chart course wider more wonderfully welcoming waters all connected confluence.

Celebrate the Ever Unfolding You- Through patient personal seasons savoring soulfulness delivering differently timed direction depending chapter context, uphold faith fluidity fashioning future freer by courage loving today.

Tomorrow's terrain remains ripe revelation embodied through you and me as we walk pilgrim pathway paved by resilience legacy exceeding limits once deemed undefiable. By their courage, ours codified overcoming. With radical self-love rooted by rivers below rerouting when Aristotle's mountains of morality moved persevering pride mined from Bedrock into beacons, take trust transformation builds beyond barriers in due time this tyranny too passes patient revolutionaries stand ground awaiting awakening one unconditional heart at a time.

Onward, inward, upward always through each trench we traverse emerging every round more boldly as our own loving liberators leading multitudes into equanimity's era where legislation lifts truth no temporal thought prison may steal away ever built withstand the brilliant bride rainbow resilience ever rising within wisely without wavering validity valued at highest summits hallowed once leveled loving lens finally focus forward teaming toward more equitable terrain promised awaiting all awakened hands and hearts uniting job freedom songs still yet unsung but destined lift many marching on melody's mighty crescendos cascading courage carrying through sustained self-love first reclaiming calm within by loving spirit perfectly as you are then awakening outward ever onward indivisibly.

5

Slaying Stereotypes: Unleashing the Power of Uniqueness

Recognizing and Challenging Stereotypes

At first rainbow hues welding symbols singularly as emblems around LGBTQ+ life liberated visibility victories decades denied. But broad brushstrokes risk relegating intricate identities into monolithic caricature corners when nuance narrows. Behind bold branding often susceptible stereotyping whole groups along generalization fault lines, individuals yearn freedom framing their own fluid stories beyond imposed tropes.

Through complex personal journeys navigating external biases about intersectional essence coded culturally, queer individuals endure bombardment by myths that fracture fuller selves straddling both celebration and grievance around marginalized membership pricing identity daily. Dogmas demarcating narrow normalcies invisibilize vibrant diversity demonstrated by multitudes embodying and loving lenses exceeding reductive stereotypes weaponized now mainstream representations uplifted initially aiming equality rhetoric but risk limiting liberty just the same.

So through these pages we will gently explode caricatures fused through sensational media, institutional doctrine and interpersonal ignorance missing multitudes thriving at identity margins beyond limiting cliches. By honoring harm hallmarks of bias perpetrate personally and politically, empathy expands upholding intricacy inherent across shared human terrain too complex conform labeling logic alone. Wisdom awakens celebrating exceptional stories success found refuting snapshots slivers when spotlit singly failed ever frame fully dynamic journeys within LGBTQ+ life thriving today.

Onward charting courses beyond constraining categories awash newly inclusive currents gradually eroding facades that fools gold fast become archaic artifacts of eras awaiting awakening. Let rainbow resonate increasingly Prismatic patterns we each uniquely kaleido-scopically configure carrying contrast and color channeling communal change.

Deconstructing LGBTQ+ Stereotypes

Behind the rainbow's refracted rays rippling unified for visibility and human rights justice, intricate intersections of identity thriving remain vulnerable caricature by those clinging heteronormative hegemony. Homogenized tropes crystallizing around singular stories frequently flood famously ahead pursuing complex dynamic community now entering spotlight after enduring generations silenced or severed from safety, security and sociopolitical citizenship.

As consciousness expands upholding equity, understanding how stereotypes falsify diversity's brilliance assists eliminating ignorance embedded historically while elevating empowered personal narratives long overlooked underfunded. Let's contextualize frequent fallacies foisted upon multifaceted LGBTQ+ people perpetuating harm often unrealized.

Gender Expression Clichés

"All tomboys become trans men. All effeminate boys mature gay" assumes gender identity and sexuality spectrums symmetrically align when millions mix match preferences fluidly across morphing contexts defying dogma. Pediatric development research by **Dr Cynthia Shame** concludes less than 15% children exhibiting strong gender expansive interests undergoes medical transition later while 25% percent identify cis hetero, disproving parental panic presumption playing princess predicts puberty blockers must follow.

"Queer aesthetics degrade work ethic and intelligence" festered when even conspicuously nonconforming thinkers like Gore Vidal and Alan Turing endured scrutiny around brilliant contributions over identity deviance by McCarthyist moralism. Corporate America concessions allowing casual attire still censor self expression freedom significant enough sustain market advantage and branding. **Dr. Angel Ng** studies workplace discrimination experiences professional trans women facing barriers mobility and compensation not cis women peers when exclusively work products equally excel.

"Nonbinary identities never existed before internet invented attention seeking self diagnoses" ignores global indigenous communities recognizing third third gender two-spirit traditions centuries predating western psychiatry's pathologization anything beyond rigid binaries. **Anthropologist Dr. Anne Bolin's** 20-year research traces hundreds artifacts art and literature celebrating gender diversity across ancient eastern/American cultures erased violently by white imperialist colonialism before recently resurfacing rights language developed defend difference again diagnostically.

Sexuality Stereotypes

"Bisexual people just can't decide. Greedy sex fiends unwilling commit." Reductive readings rob nuance that attraction manifold dimensions exists anyone anywhere a given fluidity spectrum. Monosexual assumptions mislabel like lacking integrity or self control those embracing ethical non-monogamy consensually. In reality a majority LGBTQ people report occasional opposite sex attraction disproving dogma cites steadfast separatism.

"All lesbians loathe men. Gay men all Misogynists. Trans individuals obsessed reinforcing stereotypes" Polarization politics projects internal toxicity intergroup especially when systems selectively suppressing any faction as scapegoat. In truth shared oppression carved natural alliances empathizing intersecting injustices though occasional clashes highlight homework healing hurt history sowed suspicion not innate truth people's essence equal above ignorant tropes eligibility humanity itself ever being tied behavior always mercurial by nature.

"Asexual or aromantic identities require fixing frigidity." Acephobic assumptions medicalize lack sexual/romantic attraction inherently unhealthy disorder somehow genetically problematic requiring treatment when millions find fulfilling bonding meaningful lives without coital connections convention commands. **Dr. Angela Chen** sociological research traces a-spec legitimacy across eras astrology orientations noting culpable are environments commodifying intimate bonds transactionally as sole source life purpose worth when meaning multidimensional beyond bedroom binaries.

"LGBTQ = White epidemic" While privilege visibility patterns prioritized particular palatable versions queerness primetime largely sanitizing rainbow through choice binaries characteristics, queer color always catalyzed justice from savage garden raids Emmett

Till hate murder martyring initiating civil rights, to trans women color commanding frontlines Stonewall breakthroughs survivors today driving discourse intersectionality uplifting ongoing inequity compounding racism's risks queer/trans marginalized face.

Assumption Antidotes

Literature uplifting outlier success stories stimulates empathy decoding difference ratios reality rarely observed mainstream. When media markets singular samples identity as representative universal norms, misinformation jeopardizes groups historically marginalized for holding heritages and behaviors deemed deviant by limited lenses.

Dr. Carnell Cooper's analysis urges "wholistic storytelling celebrating spectrums diverse embodiments and experiences that existed eternally through every era albeit often dangerously underground." Cooper concludes: "By exposing multitudes living loudly loving beyond plausibility plots mass consciousness conceived confined, compassion builds beneficiaries bigger boldness while bonding broader humanity."

Embracing Diversity Within the LGBTQ+ Community

The LGBTQ+ community encompasses a rich diversity of identities, experiences, and expressions. At the core, this community is about embracing our shared humanity and seeking equity, acceptance, and justice. However, within the LGBTQ+ umbrella there are also important differences that contribute unique beauty, vibrancy and strength.

In celebrating Pride, we must be intentional about lifting up the voices and stories across the full spectrum of the community. **A recent study by researchers Lisa Diamond and Clifford Rosky at the University of Utah** found that bisexual individuals often feel invisible within LGBTQ+ spaces. Meanwhile, a **survey by LaRon Nelson at the University of Rochester** revealed that transgender people and people of color disproportionately face discrimination and violence even within the community.

By sharing stories that embrace the totality of LGBTQ+ experiences, we showcase the community's richness. Hearing about people figuring themselves out, falling in love, raising children, pursuing careers, and aging—while also facing distinct challenges because of their identity—humanizes the diversity within the community. As writer and activist **Audre Lorde** stated, "It is not our differences that divide us. It is our inability to recognize, accept, and celebrate those differences."

Gender Diversity

The experiences of transgender and non-binary individuals reveal important truths about the complexity of gender. **A study by Kristina Olson at the University of Washington** found that children begin grasping their own gender identity between ages 3 and 5, demonstrating that our inner sense of self develops early. Transgender people remind us that gender encompasses more than just the sex we are assigned at birth. Their journeys to live as their authentic selves require incredible courage and resilience.

Meanwhile, people identifying outside the gender binary as non-binary, genderfluid, or gender expansive show that gender can be more complicated than just man or woman. They prompt society to move beyond restrictive boxes to embrace the full spectrum of gender identity and expression. Sharing stories about the human struggles around understanding gender gives insight and encouragement to those facing similar journeys.

Racial Diversity

LGBTQ+ people of color navigate intersectional identities, facing combined discrimination. A **report by Pakistan-born researcher Khawaja Idrees at the University of Toronto** revealed that queer immigrant youth often feel isolated and unsupported as they navigate family, culture, and sexual identity. Similarly, **a survey led by researcher Tangela Roberts at Western Michigan University** showed that LGBTQ+ people of color experience higher rates of homelessness, poverty, violence, and workplace discrimination compared to white LGBTQ+ people.

To build a strong, united community we must lift up the voices of LGBTQ+ people of color and stand beside them. hearing stories from queer Black Lives Matter activists or profiles of pioneering LGBTQ+ elected officials of color spotlights their resilient leadership. Celebrating Pride means celebrating the diversity of heritage, culture, and experience within the LGBTQ+ community.

Generational Diversity

LGBTQ+ history reminds us of how the environment facing queer individuals has evolved across generations. Older members of the community faced enormous stigma and danger simply for living openly. YOUnger generations have benefitted from those who advocated for acceptance and legal protections. However, they still face hatred and discrimination in different forms.

Sharing intergenerational stories allows for connection, empathy and solidarity across ages. For example, a **photography project by Debbie Bimbi at San Francisco State University's Center for Research and Education on Gender and Sexuality** highlighted decades-long relationships between older lesbian and gay couples. Such stories honor enduring love while showcasing a little-seen demographic within the LGBTQ community.

Meanwhile hearing from LGBTQ+ youth spotlights their unique generational challenges. A 2021 survey by the **Trevor Project led by researcher Amy Green demonstrated** alarmingly high rates of suicidal ideation among LGBTQ+ youth. Providing space for young people's voices promotes support and understanding across generations.

Religious Diversity

LGBTQ+ individuals from faith backgrounds often feel torn between their religious and sexual identity. However, many have found peace by focusing on the welcoming, compassionate teachings within their faith rather than dogmatic ideologies. Groups like Muslims for Progressive Values or organizations like Keshet supporting LGBTQ+ Jews showcase religious diversity within the community.

Sharing stories about reconciliation between religious and LGBTQ+

identities can offer hope and inspiration. Profile pieces of same-sex couples finding acceptance within their church provides an image of inclusive faith. Likewise, highlighting LGBTQ+ pastors, rabbis and other religious leaders sets an example. Relating stories where religious communities show unconditional love for LGBTQ+ members promotes a message of faith, hope and unity.

Neurodiversity & Disability Representation

LGBTQ+ individuals are represented across the spectrums of neurodiversity and disability. Those within the community who also identify as neurodiverse, such as on the autism spectrum, or as having sensory, emotional, intellectual or physical disabilities navigate complex layers of identity.

An ethnographic study led by Scott D. Johnson at the University of California Los Angeles (UCLA) found that LBGTQ+ youth with learning disabilities face compounded challenges with self-esteem, relationships and accessing community supports. Meanwhile disabled trans individuals reveal the interplay between conceptions of "normalcy" related to both ableist and cisgender norms.

Embracing and giving voice to neurodiverse and disabled narratives spotlights often marginalized identities within the LGBTQ+ community. Pride provides the opportunity to celebrate the resilience of those at intersectional frontiers - facing stigma due to both disability and LGBTQ+ identity. Advocating for accessibility and inclusion promotes solidarity rooted in embracing all kinds of minds and bodies.

Tools for Challenging Stereotypes

The Harm of Stereotypes

Stereotypes reduce diverse human experiences into oversimplified categorizations. As author **Chimamanda Ngozi Adichie cautioned in her TED talk, "The Danger of a Single Story,"** stereotypes foster misunderstanding by telling only one, often distorted side of a complex narrative.

Within the LGBTQ+ community, stereotypes reinforce stigma, marginalization and self-doubt. From depictions of flamboyant gay men to predatory lesbians - these caricatures deny the humanity behind queer identities. Ultimately, **dismantling destructive stereotypes** requires education, open dialogue, and intentional efforts toward mutual understanding.

The Power of Education

Education expands perspectives, reveals shared struggles, and connects lived experiences. An impactful **2013 study by Jeremy David Garrett at Indiana University** demonstrated how a semester-long intergroup dialogue course significantly reduced prejudicial attitudes between LGBTQ+ individuals and religious students. Facilitated exchange of stories shifted attitudes by humanizing those from disparate social groups.

On an individual level, seeking out books, films, art and media created by LGBTQ+ people provides insight into the real diversity of queer narratives. Attending pride parades and festivals offers exposure - putting faces and voices to a community that defies one-dimensional stereotypes. Or engaging personal connections with LGBTQ+ friends and family fosters empathy and growth.

Meanwhile from a young age, inclusive curriculum and sex education helps mitigate harmful stereotypes about gender and sexuality. Teaching youth to critically analyze media portrayals allows them to become conscientious, discerning consumers of information. Education in all forms expands understanding which is the first step to addressing unfair stereotypes.

The Gift of Open Dialogue

Open, non-judgmental dialogue provides space for sharing authentic stories and clearing up misconceptions. **Researchers Susan Burgess and Sally Kuykendall at the University of San Francisco** studied structured "story circle" groups bringing LGBTQ+ youth together with police officers. Candid personal storytelling shifted attitudes, reduced youth distrust, and even improved neighborhood climate.

Creating space for dialogue starts with asking open-ended questions then genuinely listening to understand - not just react. Workers can organize voluntary discussion groups with LGBTQ+ colleagues to learn about their experiences. Teachers might facilitate respectful debate around gender diversity issues to expand student perspectives.

Where tensions arise from hurtful language or stereotypical depictions, avoid immediate condemnation. Instead engage in constructive dialogue to uncover and address underlying attitudes. **Extensive studies by prejudice reduction trainer Jane Elliot** reveal that confrontation often reinforces defensiveness whereas non-judgmental exchange builds self-awareness and capacity for change.

While sometimes uncomfortable, leaning into nuanced dialogue around complex issues paves the path for mutual understanding and reducing stereotypes.

The Unifying Force of Allyship

Allies who stand in solidarity alongside marginalized groups foster humanization that dissolves stereotypes. Even small acts like wearing rainbow pins or putting preferred gender pronouns in email signatures signals support and welcoming spaces for LGBTQ+ people.

Research by Tiffany Jones and Gabriel Merrin at the Human Rights Campaign Foundation shows that LGBTQ+ students feel safer and more engaged in schools with Gender and Sexuality Alliance Clubs and outward signs of inclusion from staff. Similarly, workplaces that celebrate Pride month help employees bring their authentic selves to work reducing anxiety and stereotype threat.

Meanwhile straight and cisgender allies can lend their voices to LGBTQ+ initiatives providing credibility from outside the community. A **study by Rachel Wagner at the University of North Texas** revealed that school antibullying policies were more impactful when student allies were actively involved not just marginalized youth alone. Allies standing in solidarity along LGBTQ+ peers warms social climates for openness, understanding and reduction of unfair stereotypes.

Create Space for LGBTQ+ Voices

Ultimately, the most impactful tool for challenging stereotypes lies in making space for LGBTQ+ voices to share the uniqueness, diversity and relatability of queer stories. Uplifting authentic narratives in media, literature, research and personal circles conveys richness within the community defying limiting stereotypes.

Even spotlighting the prominence of LGBTQ+ individuals across professions challenges assumptions - whether scientists, soldiers, celebrities or politicians. Showcasing excellence and perseverance proves sexual orientation and gender identity irrelevant to human goals and contributions.

Recognition of shared dreams and struggles touches hearts and opens minds. The humanity shining through unfiltered LGBTQ+ stories holds transformational power to dispel myths and bring communities together. For when we relate person to person, labels and stereotypes fade allowing our universal essence to connect.

Turning Stereotypes into Strengths

Reclaiming Agency Over Definitions

Marginalized groups often face negative stereotypes seeking to demean, restrict or demonize. Rather than internalize these limiting narratives, many within the LGBTQ+ community have reclaimed power by boldly embracing qualities ascribed to them.

With pride and self-assurance, they stand tall in who they are - subverting stereotypes designed to attack their dignity. By redefining and reorienting labels, they harness presumed "weaknesses" into sources of empowerment and social change.

Flipping the Script on Effeminacy

Stereotypes around effeminate speech and mannerisms in gay men aim to emasculate and portray inferior status. However trailblazers like gender non-conforming performer **RuPaul Charles** have gained global influence by unabashedly celebrating feminized expression.

With glamorous flair in drag combined with power vocal messages like "If you don't love yourself, how in the hell you gonna love somebody else?" RuPaul models self-acceptance and advocacy. Other public figures like Billy Porter turn heads on red carpets wearing gowns and high heels, expanding social conceptions of masculinity.

Even the Progressive Insurance ads starring "Flo" played by actor **Leslie Jordan** leaned into stereotypes around the flamboyant gay man. However Jordan's warm, likeable character ultimately projects positivity and mass appeal. By boldly asserting one's right to gender transgression, these pioneers claimed ownership over qualities used to denigrate them.

Embracing Nonconformist Identities

Bisexual, pansexual, non-binary and other emerging identities within the LGBTQ+ spectrum defy conformity around societal expectations. However openness around complex, shifting and fluid identities bravely confronts convention.

Pop performer **Miley Cyrus**, a visible advocate for LGBTQ+ communities, identifies as pansexual gender-nonconforming. By expressing refusal to box one's self into defined labels, Cyrus role models self-assurance for those questioning societal rules around attraction and expression.

Non-binary and gender non-conforming activists use visibility in roles like public office as Chicago City Alderperson Matt Martin or leader of the Ontario Federation of Labour **Siobhan Hardwick** to increase acceptance of those living outside traditional gender norms. Rather than hide nonconforming orientations, proudly embracing these identities bursts through restrictive stereotypes.

Subverting Expectations About Discrimination

A common narrative depicts LGBTQ+ individuals as inherently marginalized victims lacking power. However increasing numbers openly celebrate their identity while gaining influence across high-profile domains like business, law, faith communities and politics.

For example, the former CEO of Apple **Tim Cook** willingly addressed his sexuality saying he considers it "a gift from God" not an impediment to wild success in tech. Meanwhile pastor and author **Megan Rohrer** became the first openly transgender American bishop within the Evangelical Lutheran church.

By succeeding in spaces historically less accepting of LGBTQ+ identities, these trailblazers subvert expectations of repression and powerlessness. Their presence expands perceived realms of opportunity for those who identify similarly. They boldly claim power and acceptance in places where once only discrimination may have existed.

Comedic Commentary Claiming Power

The coping mechanism of using humor to call out oppression has offered subversive relief within minority groups for ages. Building on this tradition, contemporary queer comedians irreverently use sharp wit to expose and ridicule societal prejudice around LGBTQ+ stereotyping.

Gay stand up comic **Tig Notaro** elevated comedy as power with her famous set where she boldly stripped stereotypes and stigmas by announcing, "Good evening. Hello. I have cancer. How are you?" This jarring punchline throwing the audience turned societal discomfort with illness and "otherness" into laughable absurdity.

Similarly **Hannah Gadsby's** groundbreaking standup special "Nanette" provided searing cultural commentary around being a gender non-conforming lesbian in a world still rampant with homophobia and sexism. The profound impact comes through using humor and personal narrative to highlight injustice then flip the script into bold commentary.

By weaponizing stereotype-derived assumptions against the oppressors, these pioneering comedians reclaim dignity, empowerment and cultural influence. Their brazen humor fosters healing catharsis while eroding rigid constraints around societal inclusion and mobility.

Unleashing Your Unique Power

In reviewing diverse stories across the vibrant spectrum of LGBTQ+ identity, a unifying message emerges. At the core, embracing our authentic selves and refusing to conform to limiting stereotypes is truly what unleashes the full force of our human potential.

By boldly championing qualities, behaviors or lifestyles outside perceived societal "norms," these courageous individuals convert scorned difference into rising power. Their defiant pride in self-definition subverts limiting narratives opening doors for mass shift around embracing uniqueness without judgment.

What conventional wisdom may malign as "other," marginalized groups reclaim as sacred ground for revealing humanity's diversity. By spotlighting voices from the sexual, racial or gender frontiers – insight emerges that complexity and fluidity define identity more than static generalizations. As we raise up nuanced stories reflecting shared hopes yet wide-ranging individuality, mutual understanding dispels the myth of "normal" making space to honor each person's distinct essence and talents.

Redefining "Normal"

In truth, the entire spectrum of human experience holds normalcy and worthiness. Just as a pride parade weaves together many colors, backgrounds and modes of expression - the inclusion of all creates vibrant beauty. From cisgender to transgender, disabled to athletic, highly educated to creative innovator – every variation carries value in composing humanity's diverse mosaic.

Stereotypes targeting those who identify or present differently aim to dehumanize groups who don't conform. However embracing the totality of identity bestows unsilenceable dignity while unveiling gifts inside each person. By proudly championing qualities society may label as weaknesses, marginalized individuals reveal the subjectivity underlying restrictive beliefs around norms. They courageously explode myths by excelling in spheres from which they were excluded, shifting culture to recognize the arbitrary boundaries drawn by convention.

Free to Define Your Own Story

In managing our personal journey, key insights emerge to guide next steps:

First, refuse false dichotomies. Few aspects of human experience truly occupy absolute categories without overlap or exceptions. Do not force yourself into narrow boxes with blurry boundaries rendered meaningless under close inspection. You possess full authority to identify however best fits your authentic self even if vague societal rules protest.

Second, let no one else define your capabilities based on identity. Ability, talent and possibility live across all demographics and per-sonality types. Pay no mind to those claiming you cannot achieve milestones because of superficial qualities. The only limits are those we place upon ourselves by believing others' limiting projections.fab

Third, embrace fluidity and change as you move through life's seasons. Growth requires progressively shedding ill-fitting skins to emerge renewed after struggle. Do not cling to previous versions of identity if your inner truth shifts directions or expands perspectives. Flow with your personal evolution without judgment.

Finally, lift your voice to accelerate acceptance for others still struggling to confidently champion their uniqueness in the face of stigma. Your lived experience holds power and credibility to foster radical compassion in wider society. Share your whole story to model possibility for outcasts and outliers crushed under weighty stereotypes. For in bonding together pride lifts all to higher ground beyond WASPy norms that fail to encompass or celebrate the breadth of humanity.

Building an Inclusive Culture

Moving forward individually and collectively, honoring each person's distinct qualities and perspectives clears ground for innovative breakthrough. Just as biodiversity fortifies resilient ecosystems, embracing the mosaic of human identities, ideologies, neurotypes and orientations strengthens our social fabric to solve complex problems.

Progress relies on pushing boundaries, listening without judgment and standing in solidarity with the marginalized. By openly addressing limiting biases and dismantling systems favoring conformity, we blast through artificial constraints on human potential. From the ashes, space emerges for new societal structures that honor each individual while empowering diverse cooperative communities.

The hour has arrived for radical celebration of uniqueness as a guiding light through dark tunnels of oppression. Pride marches forward as love and fierce compassion dissolve the fences separating gay from straight, black from white, typical from impaired. Here stands the integrated human family in all its peculiar glory! When people unite to uphold every member's intrinsic right to champion their distinctive essence free from hierarchy or exploitation, that day oppression gasps its last.

May we tear down reductive stereotypes and social barriers separating minority groups from the mainstream. As we open eyes to see, souls to feel and minds to understand beyond suffocating boxes, space materializes for revolutionary concepts of "normal". Through the lens of inclusion celebrating outlier voices, we collectively give birth to a new social paradigm rooted in the truth – that empowerment and unity bloom most beautifully when each person nurtures their distinctive bloom.

So unleash yourself fully with head high and middle fingers at society's conventions. Wave your freak flag high as the pioneering LGBTQ+ community models. For diversity stands as humanity's life raft through swirling tides of change. Our collective difference and willingness to champion one another defiantly in the face of conformity is what will carry all people to freedom's shore.

6

Coming Out Confetti: Celebrating Your Truth

The Ongoing Journey of Coming Out

"Coming out" holds monumental significance as both a single step and lifelong process within the shared experience of identifying as LGBTQ+. Declaring one's authentic sexual orientation, gender identity, or mere questioning plunges open the doorway between inner truth and outer reality. By crossing the threshold to reveal a long-hidden essence to others, space emerges to begin living freely as one's integrated whole self.

Yet the decision to disclose an identity straying from societal "norms" given the lingering stigma and ignorance requires incredible courage and vulnerability. Each coming out instance contains risk and unpredictable consequences. However, sharing one's personal story audaciously chips away at stereotypes through humanizing LGBTQ+ experiences as familiar human struggles around identity and belonging.

Ultimately, the power of coming out appears less in isolated incidents of revealing guarded secrets and more through the ongoing unfolding of truth seeking continual understanding and acceptance. Every coming out moment makes space for more people, particularly youth, to brave the journey toward self-acceptance and authentic expression. And with more diverse stories kindling awareness and empathy, society progresses toward inclusion.

Coming Out as an Expression of Soul

Beyond mere statements of fact around one's sexual or gender identity, at its core coming out expresses a spiritual choice – the commitment to live aligned with soulful essence rather than externally-imposed expectations. Beneath surface declarations around being lesbian, gay, bisexual, transgender or any queer identity, coming out proclaims:

"I know my personal truth. Despite society resisting, I accept myself fully. I refuse conditioned shame, unworthiness or pressure to conform. I honor my inner wisdom above the ignorance of others."

In its mystical form, coming out means awakening to love one's whole self unconditionally despite lingering doubts or detractors. It celebrates the hard-won self-awareness to emerge from the chrysalis of confusion into luminous integrity. Coming out embodies the soulful act of blossoming into wholeness under the warmth of self-acceptance.

This holds as a lifelong process of continually shedding limiting shells in each growth phase to manifest more completely. At core, the potency of living openly relies not on any label but rather the self-honoring mindset upholding, "I matter, and I will allow no one else's discomfort with my identity to dim my light again."

No Single Moment Defines Completion

While society generally discusses coming out as a one-time event or milestone, in reality the continual emergence of living authentically never ceases even once you fully inhabit the truth of identity. Each coming summer invites new adventures toward self-expression just as the cyclical nature of plants persist in pushing out fresh buds each season.

Comedian and talk show host Ellen Degeneres shares that even 20 years after publicly coming out on her sitcom's 1997 episode, then seeing her career nosedive before rising to success again, she still moves through ongoing evolution around being comfortable discussing her identity. She emphasizes, "It's a process. It's an evolution."

In her 2017 memoir, "The Bold World," transgender author Jodie Patterson reflects, "There is always more of myself to come out to." She reveals that despite surgically transitioning years back, she continually experiences revelations around unpacking shame, dismantling internalized oppression and settling more wholly into her being.

Within the journey of integrating one's wholeness, each stage of coming out reinforces courage and self-trust. With practice emerges confidence to fully inhabit your being however that manifests in the world. But fixed completion points prove elusive when living means continually outgrowing shells to reveal your essence anew.

The Ripple Effects from Speaking Openly

While excising secrecy and repression grants the gift of aligning outer life with inner truths, coming out also powerfully impacts spheres far beyond the individual. Revelation of personal stories fosters waves of awareness raising, political activation and unity building advancing

LGBTQ+ culture shifting.

Gill Foundation's National Coming Out project highlights how nearly everyone today knows a person who identifies openly as LGBTQ+ while 20 years ago acquaintances stayed closeted. They emphasize that personal familiarity holds the power to transform attitudes and build acceptance exponentially across communities. Support for LGBTQ+ protections nearly doubles when people realize loved ones directly benefit.

And historically, pivotal coming out moments sparked momentum and visibility for the movement overall. Whether celebrities like Ellen or athletes like Jason Collins in the NBA declaring their queer identity, politicians fighting for representation, or trans authors and academics boldly publishing research - every out person normalizes LGBTQ+ experiences across diverse demographics. Eventually unfamiliar begins blending into familiar.

On a sociopolitical level, researchers confirm that LGBTQ+ in-dividuals actively volunteering, financial contributing and lobbying politicians advances rights for the marginalized at-large. By personally coming out, power activates on individual and collective levels to drive systemic change. All from the seemingly simple, yet infinitely courageous act of communicating one's authentic self to the world ardently longing to understand.

So while the milestone moments merit celebration for those new to living openly, coming out's effects ripple so much further. Each story plants seeds toward justice. Each life lifted up pulls others still struggling from despair's pit toward the light of self-love. No act of courageous honesty wasted but rather contributing to collective emancipation.

And with radical pride the LGBTQ+ community models for all people that pathways toward liberation emerge by boldly shedding limiting expectations until your full humanity shines bright enough to warm even the coldest of hearts. The personal journey toward self-love fuels fiery passion strengthening bonds across diversity to raise the consciousness of the whole. Out and proud, change unfolds one story at a time!

Understanding the Coming-Out Process

While no two coming out journeys unfold exactly alike, many share common milestones and challenges along the winding path toward living openly. By understanding the emotional stages, risks and opportunities of exploring and declaring an LGBTQ+ identity, we can offer greater empathy and support loved ones navigating coming out.

Waking Up to Identity

Coming out starts with inward exploration toward acknowledging, naming and accepting one's identity which may not align with heteronormative expectations. For some this manifests in childhood sensory awareness or budding adolescent attractions. For others the recognition dawns slowly over years, even entering relationships that disguise one's orientation.

According to human development models by psychologist **Vivienne Cass**, the early stage of identity awareness generates confusion and emotional turmoil. Facing an identity shrouded in cultural stigma often ignites profound feelings of alienation, shame and fear around being viewed as abnormal or deviant. Attempts to deny, change or rationalize away homosexual/transgender feelings generally fail providing temporary relief.

Over time however, increasing information through books, media and internet community enables LGBTQ+ individuals to better understand experiences as part of a shared social phenomenon rather than isolated perversion. Finding positive role models and terminology to describe feelings allows self-esteem to strengthen. Eventually identity becomes understood not as problem needing correction but discovery of truthful self.

Weighing Self-Disclosure

Once embracing one's identity as beautiful discovery rather than troublesome affliction, the epic question emerges around whether or not to reveal this inner world to others through coming out. As students from Macquarie University in Sydney, Australia revealed in a qualitative study led by **Dr. Tiffany Jones**, for marginalized groups "the personal still very much becomes political." Deliberations weigh heavy with social implications.

On the one hand, coming out offers relief of authentic self-expression without carrying exhausting lies. Living openly also allows access to relationships and LGBTQ+ community missed by hiding. Newfound boldness emerges from reclaiming agency to define oneself.

However coming out rarely guarantees unilateral acceptance, especially among conservative family cultures. Severe reactions may jeopardize financial/social support critical for wellbeing. Without cultural progress secured, much still hinges on individual reception. For youth especially, coming out means assuming real risks given dependence on potentially unsupportive people. Navigating disclosure conversations requires careful strategy.

Emerging Into Openness

If adequate confidence builds in readiness to share inner truth despite associated vulnerabilities, coming out unfolds through direct conversation or subtle hints allowing others to gradually deduce identity. Ideally coming out moves into a phase of integrating openness into all aspects of life, not cordoning it away as disjointed secret.

Still, coming out rarely concludes after a single disclosure event as new settings continuously require deciding whether to reveal minority status. Longterm LGBTQ+ individuals emphasize needing to deliberately come out repeatedly when meeting new colleagues, healthcare providers, neighbors and acquaintances. Identity persists needing practical protection through continually assessing safety with newly introduced individuals.

Together the external steps toward socially manifesting internal identity shifts carve the coming out journey. Not necessarily linear but more spiral, with forward momentum interspersed by emotional setbacks yet continually looping upward over time. What originated internally settles with boldness into daily life as part of one's integrated personality. Pride emerges from owning all of oneself.

Navigating Family Reactions

American University researchers **Bil Leipold and Andrew Greve** identify coming out within family life as uniquely challenging yet critical. They emphasize families establish human's earliest sense of belonging. Their beginnings shore up foundations for identity. When identity later conflicts with family systems, painful dissonance results.

Ideally family relationships offer refuge for understanding and encouragement toward self-definition throughout coming out struggles. But impressions of rejection or condemnation from closest loved ones cuts profoundly. Conversion therapy practices by unaccepting families exacerbate harm by attempting to reorient LGBTQ individuals' core being.

With acceptance, family bonds grow enriched through honesty conveying deepest essence beneath surface roles. However even in worst case scenarios, initiating a self-honoring path forward remains vital. Constructing "families of choice" within LGBTQ+ community secures essential mirrors for seeing own cherished belonging. Walking the path openly aligns footsteps toward living whole.

Trust Your Own Timing

Psychologist **Dr. Caitlin Ryan's** Family Acceptance Project emphasizes only the LGBTQ+ individuals themselves can determine correct pacing for coming out. Particularly for youth dependent on family resources for housing and education, risks require reasonable safety planning.

By first coming out to trusted allies able to provide emotional or literal shelter if needed, safety nets establish for the road ahead. But no perfect formula guarantees outcomes since reactions prove highly personal. Ultimately each journey must follow inner wisdom balancing timing with available spiritual and tangible support.

Navigating Different Coming-Out Experiences

While the landmarks of exploring celentity, assessing safety, initially disclosing, then integrating openness characterize common phases of coming out, individual experiences navigate these steps in enormously diverse ways. Age, culture, religion, disability status, along with idiosyncrasies of personality and circumstances yield unique stories.

By showcasing the range of adventures toward living openly across the LGBTQ+ spectrum, we cultivate compassion for the emotional complexity around manifesting inner selves outwardly. We dispel simply stereotypes through conveying real humanity struggling shared battles for authenticity and belonging.

Elliot: Coming Out as Transgender

Elliot (formerly Ellen) Page recently shared his coming out journey as transgender through an emotional Instagram post and cover story interview with Time Magazine. He expressed knowing from childhood, "I wanted to be a boy," cutting hair short and being mistaken for a boy even by strangers. However growing up before wide transgender visibility or role models, confusion and shame overwhelmed true identity understanding.

Desire to be an actor complicated feelings given ladies enjoyed more interesting roles and societal privileges. So Ellen embodied those female acting parts suppressing personal discomforts below career ambitions. But undeniable distress increasingly emerged being labeled woman/lesbian externally but never aligning internally.

After coming out as lesbian years prior, praise for bravery felt dishonest to Elliot harboring these deeper untruths. Only through later transgender visibility did concepts arise explaining decades of anguish. As Page processed realizing, "Oh my God...I'm trans, that's who I am," sudden self-perception shifted. He underwent surgical transition to physically affirm gender identity, immediately relieving dysphoria struggles.

While today expressing profound alignment in identity and self-love, Elliot says he feels only at the beginning stages of coming out now embracing living genuinely as his whole authentic self. He less came out once than continues progressing through stages of revelation and settling into bold transgender empowerment.

Gabrielle: Coming Out in Religious Family

When Gabrielle first acknowledged attraction toward a close friend in middle school, panic flooded attempting suppression and bargaining with God to take these feelings away. Raised in traditional Catholic household, homophobic slurs like "You're so gay!" stabbed casually throughout childhood. Implications revolved around being gay somehow making one less worthy of rights or God's love.

Tormented by escalating desires toward women despite the overt messaging that homosexuality violated nature, Gabrielle dove fervently into faith efforts praying the gay away. She attended religious conference where speakers promised sexual conversion. For awhile distracting herself through excessive devotion provided relief by redirecting thoughts outward rather than confronting inner truth.

Over years however, persistent attractions fused with questions around why God would allow gays to exist yet condemn their capacity to love. Through soul-searching and online commune with others facing similar struggles, her views shifted from internalized oppression toward self-affirmation around all paths of ethical love holding dignity. She eventually professed sexuality to close friends who offered loving support.

In young adulthood, Gabrielle gathered courage to come out to family. Mixed reactions ensued with her mother demonstrating loving reassurance versus father's stern warnings to stay silent or face exclusion from church activities still holding community importance. Today she navigates staying devoted to Christianity that uplifted childhood while forging space to honor personal identity once condemned. The journey continues needing navigation between spiritual safety and authentic expression.

Lin: Coming Out Across Cultures

Asian cultures infuse coming out complexes between strong cultural views around family honor and shame versus emerging individualism. For Chinese American Lin, understanding identity meant unraveling constricting views that homosexuals somehow failed traditions by not continuing family ancestral lines or properly attending elders.

Furthermore sacrifices from immigrant parents to secure privileges like Lin's US citizenship and college education instilled immense Pressure to become the perfect performing child in return, implicitly requiring hiding any parts deemed culturally deviant. Even language gaps estranged building trust to share vulnerable realities across generations.

Initial coming out to progressive college friends offered temporary relief through new "family" support. But fears accelerated nearing graduation requiring either confronting conservative parents or living indefinitely wearing disguises to appease them. After months withdrawn in isolation, Lin attempted suicide strained by the weight of denial and dishonesty corroding inner wholeness.

In glimpsing permanent loss, family traveled overseas visiting Lin's hospital bedside aware something demanded embracing beyond surface cultural rules. Through extended dialogue and education among local LGBTQ+ Asian groups, they progressed accepting Lin's identity even while navigating discomforts. Together the journey continues toward bridging culture divides to fully integrate Lin's wholeness back into the family fold.

No Single Path but All Walk With Courage

As diverse as snowflakes, coming out stories traverse unique cultural intersections, sacrifices, awakenings and embodiments of profound truth-telling. Whether plunging through paralysis of fear or gently wading outward through tides of incremental change - all who voyage toward living openly display uncommon valor and grace worthy of honor.

For inherently no "right pathway" presents clearly. We all stumble through shadows of the unknown seeking flickers signaling safe passage. In these tender liminal spaces, hands clasp together steering collective fate. Just one light kindled sparking radical self-compassion cradling outcasts to dry land delivers multitudes to more sure footing where acceptance, justice and celebration awaits.

Tools for Self-Reflection and Preparation

Despite immense diversity across coming out experiences, common ground exists around the importance of inner work enabling clarity and confidence before sharing vulnerable truths outwardly. By exploring identity more fully within, space materializes for aligning external manifestations with core essence through coming out.

Know Yourself Before Expecting Others

Coming out means unveiling intensely personal dimensions of identity often camouflaged for years. Trying skipping intermediate steps of internal self-discovery risks communication breakdowns given even you just now start digesting this unfolding revelation. How reasonably expect others to quickly comprehend your journey still fuzzy even internally?

Start coming out to yourself before facing world. Identify feelings, behaviors and visions long-buried to finally acknowledge inner landscape. Dig into shadowy spaces resisting examination. What stories or archetypes feel aligned versus areas generating friction against true self? Mapping your terrain marks footing when beckoning others toward seldom traversed paths.

Try journaling to unpack emotions, assumptions and experiences around identity. When did first glimmers of self-perceived "differentness" emerge? What societal messages imbued shame? From where did pride eventually shine vindication? Capture memories evoking identity imprints across lifespan to unveil limiting scripts and self-authored transformation truths. Know your history before rewriting next chapters.

Assess Motivations

Examine deeper drivers beckoning disclosure now when previous seasons guarded secrecy. Take inventory around intentions for coming out rather than simply reacting reflexively to identity awakenings.

Are you pursuing transparency toward living authentically, redirecting energy from hiding into dreams awaiting fuller focus? Or do motives steer closer to defiance or rebellion against externally-imposed norms no longer tolerable? Matter less what is coming out than spirit behind – shame evacuation or soul embellishment? Clarity of purpose eases navigation around consequences.

Furthermore, assess secondary gains unconsciously sought like garnering attention, nursing wounds through sympathy or liberating anger suppressed under years of conformity pressure. Such motivations potentially corrode coming out integrity by entangling validation-seeking with truth-telling. Untangling knotty impulses grants steadier footing.

Envision Your Bold Preferred Future

Beyond processing past and present, visualize preferred life directions once no longer saddled by secrecy. Allow imagination to play with identity manifestations less weighed down by other's expectations.

What authentic expressions excite previously avoided? Who becomes possible once separating external judgments from internal compass? What interests and passions now deserve nurturing freed from energy draining hiding oneself? Dare dreaming without false modesty around long-denied hopes. Through envisioning future selves liberation takes form.

This mental preparation erects scaffolding that coming out conversations merely aim filling. By first architecting structures of self-acceptance, you inhabit personal power to calmly steer dialogue even amidst resistance. When grounded know your destination, opposition proves navigable detour rather obstacle to advancement.

Assess Safety Before Proceeding

While the soul longs rushing forth unrestrained conveying most genuine identity, practical concerns around emotional and physical safety cannot dismiss when dependent on family systems still solidifying stance. Tragically conversion therapy and LGBTQ+ youth homelessness prove still far too common with vulnerable financial and legal status.

Gauge risks around housing security, educational funding and healthcare access should worst case severance occur. Only proceed sharing coming out conversations once basic stability guaranteed through personal means or reliable allies. Prioritize safety with contingency plans in place before testing waters. You can always disclose identities later but never undo fallout consequences from reacting rashly prematurely. There lies no shame only in patience prudent protecting wellness foundations until conditions allow truer vulnerability.

Inform Your Allies

Before formal coming out dialogues, discreetly inform close allies likely offering loving support. Having backup familiar with journey thus far equips hands catching unavoidable tears or tensions initial conversations unleash. Confidants help ground perspective when emotions amplify reactions. Testing coming out language also builds fluency to ease future disclosure.

Secure counselor assistance if available or connect identity affirming LGBTQ+ groups preparing best to weather challenges ahead. Gather your grace-giving team to champion likelihood of acceptance, or at minimum affirm worthiness even facing painful rejection. With trusted community cheering along the path, travels commence surer footing however scenes shift ahead. You walk into revelation already together.

Ongoing Support for Various Coming-Out Stages

While proudly sharing inner truth with loved ones marks major milestone, coming out remains ongoing journey nurturing continual support. Myriad challenges unfold integrating identity into personal relationships, professional roles and wider community navigation requiring empathy, wisdom and resilience long after initial disclosures. By building skills and solidarity networks, space holds for all to travel paths of authenticity with compassion thriving each step ahead.

Navigating Relationships Post-Coming Out

Romantic connections often first compel coming out realizations seeking expression. However relationships shift introducing external vulnerability lacking the solitary refuge of secrecy. Now another's understandings and values shape intimacy.

Early on, establish ongoing safe space for unpacking evolution around identity discoveries for both partners. Recognize sexuality and gender proving fluid, multidimensional aspects of self often unfurling gradually even through committed relationships. Assume best intent around each other's processing.

Address conflicts not as attacks but openings for deeper wisdom. Explore lovers workshops together for LGBTQ+ couples strengthening communication and alignment like those offered by relationship coach **Dr. Elisabeth Sheff**. Her research quantifies how openly negotiating agreements around monogamy versus consensual nonmonogamy, recognizing relationship transitions between friends/lovers, or flexibly supporting gender changes allows bonds trustee through turmoil. With compassion ahead challenges turn growth.

Finding Empowering Community

Visibility among empowered LGBTQ+ community provides mirrors for self-love missing within dominant cultural narratives still progressing inclusion. Whether connecting local groups, following social media voices or attending Pride events – exposure reinforces pride and resiliency. Do not isolate but lean into spaces holding lived understanding around navigating life openly.

Try volunteering with organizations elevating LGBTQ+ initiatives to simultaneously impact society while connecting personal meaningfully community. Or discoverIntersectional voices like writer **Tai Amri Spann** speaking to multiple marginalized identities with bold empowerment. Find inspiring people shattering limits on happiness or success because of identity. What feels demoralizing alone gains strength collectively uplifted.

Maintaining Mental Health

Despite liberating steps aligning outer life with inner truths, post-coming out challenges still arise like navigating career barriers, public harassment or family turbulence strained by disclosure. Sociopolitical threats also loom regarding LGBTQ+ rights rollercoasters. Building ongoing mental health practices bolsters resilience meeting recurring struggles.

Therapists specially trained in LGBTQ+ competence through associations like WPATH or AASECT offer critical support processing internalized oppression or external discrimination. Beyond therapy, creative passions soothe souls while supercharging advocacy. Literature anthologies like "The Right Side of History" compile queer activist writings countering injustice. Discover mental health sustenance then gift back inspiration.

Securing Healthy Support Networks

Remember coming out remains not checkpoint but ongoing journey revealing further dimensions of identity and self-expression. Pace personal evolution while consistently securing emotional nurturance sources and practical stability foundations.

Rather than expecting all from biological family, construct "families of choice" within communities embracing fully. Coach **Aisha Shahid** guides building intentional personal boards like having dedicated advisors around career, health or spirituality needs. Aspects unaddressed sufficiently require seeking external mentors preventively buffering depletion.

No matter how far already dared tread openly, hands still lift each other stepping ahead. Permission granted languishing when worn yet resilience regained resting together. For trailblazers shine lights so no one walks alone in darkness again. Our stories steer collective fates toward the dawn.

Celebrate Your Journey, Embrace Your Truth

The winding road of coming out traverses vastly diverse directions, speeds and terrains between individuals yet commonly leads toward profound liberation. While situations and identities constantly shift like kaleidoscopes, all who dare gaze inward then beam outwardly their unique integrated truth push collective consciousness further.

By now clearly no formula or complete map neatly predicts coming out's adventures holding intrinsic mess and magic within human vulnerability and resilience. However in reviewing others' odysseys, one's witness offers silent companionship so no story walks alone anymore. If these words ease those carrying uncertainty's weight today: let that burden lift as they boldly chart what lies ahead. For living itself means finding freedom spins faith where once only fear festered.

One should celebrate every question pondered over identity assumed predetermined. Each grip loosened from conformity's leash allows self-authored futures unfolding however fits sovereign soul. Whether disclosure leaps full-force or inches cautiously forward - respect what timing intuition knows necessary while one grows empowered inhabiting whole self.

Release false dichotomies splitting aspects eternally yearning integration. Through tears and laughter discover just how much beauty arises integrating identities once segregated. Let coming out commence not conclusively but continuously as each courageous conversation connects one more fragmented shard until beholding shimmering stained glass self.

With radically soft eyes one should perceive life's unfolding no longer burden but blessing. For when weapons word by word dismantle limiting labels and narrow notions of normal - glorious garden emerges. Gone dividing walls; come golden light redeeming outcasts. Darkness dare not breach where proud hearts bloom open toward no longer stifled horizons.

One should honor every step slow or daring, quiet or deafening, climbed by those transforming inner wilderness into haven. Your journey carves fresh tracks so others follow secreting isolated no more. May shame burn away by fiery truth-telling. When souls unite declaring "we breathe free here" - lies and violence lose grip to uphold status quo. Self-love lifts all boats floating on rising tides until washed ashore freedom's land.

So chart forward: in discomfort faith ripening, through others' reactions stand tall, with time and experience identity-clarity flows lucid as water. However path proceeds or relates with dominant views, at core celebrate the sacred gift being uniquely you. Honor emotive intricacies, gather patient allies and let intuition mentor way where clarity lacking. Build capacity carrying uncertainty as biases shift. No matter where now planted find nourishment, grow resilient. The road arises stepping beyond comfort's cage. Only by living whole one lifts the veil.

With bold vulnerability and unflappable conviction, tender hearts persist breaking cycles trapping authenticity silent. May coming out stories build bonds bridging difference into shared vision: people unapologetically ablaze stoking fires of compassion which light worlds too long left dark. For once lit within, beacon ignites revolution. Journey now brightly wherever uniqueness was once obliged hide. Blaze trail for outcasts to follow. With boldness and belonging, fear stands no chance so truth prevails.

One should celebrate the first flutters of questions cracking shells of assumed identity. Cheer fledgling attempts articulating experience long-muzzled disguising natural form. As life crescendos toward most vibrant fully-realized self beyond suffocating norms, never stop coming out. Rejoice infusing breath to the parts once obscured but now liberated shining bright blessing generations to come. The gift is receiving one's whole being, then courage offering unique full brilliance gifting those still searching mirrors revealing the beauty in simply belonging.

So come out, come out wherever you are!

7

Soundtrack to Self-Discovery

The Power of Music in Self-Discovery

Music holds unparalleled power uniting our human tapestry across cultures and eras through utterly universal languages of rhythm, melody and lyricism. Songs speak directly to the soul unlike any other artform. And for marginalized communities, music uniquely anchors ongoing quests of self-discovery and survival.

Whether chanting ceremonial drums, composing poetic ballads or mixing electronic beats – LGBTQ+ musicians encode secret messages of identity, coded history lessons,vvvv and promises of hope within artistic mediums bypassing dominant restrictions. Their rhythmic mediums slyly unwrap gifts of Pride passing under radars of prejudice.

Through lyrics and symbols coded implicitly yet profoundly understood by those similarly journeying self-exploration along society's edges - queer musicians send mirroring validation lacking within mainstream visibility. They compellingly demonstrate grappling universal themes of seeking love, purpose and freedom through a shared lens of resisting conformity.

In response, LGBTQ+ fans cling to breakthrough artists boldly expressing messages once silenced and dormant internal stirrings now declared openly. Music holds power touching marginalized lives when representation remains scarce elsewhere. Audibly hearing your story validates inner experiences raising self-esteem while driving advocacy. Famously Lady Gaga attributes LGBTQ youth contacting her around landmark track "Born This Way" say it empowered them come out, averted suicide or motivated dignity despite hardship.Radio and streaming playlists deliver musical life rafts float listeners from isolation toward community belonging.

Beyond mirroring queer experience, music also uniquely mobilizes emotional impact fueling the LGBTQ+ justice movement historically from gay anthems at the Stonewall Riots to recent youth activation. Stirring beats, chants and lyrics ignite fiery passion converging individual struggles into waves of collective change. Whether historic rallying cries or modern pride parade thumpers – music generates momentum, camaraderie and uncompromising hope rising above reactionary fear.

Finally music preserving marginalized history delivers intergenerational gifts when culture erases critical narratives. Documented accounts face censorship risks mainstream media gatekeeping. However buried in musical formats from folk to pop– tales of identity awakenings, secret love, outraged activism and pride persistence replay infinitely withstanding time and backlash. Each generation stands on melodic shoulders sharing wisdom of those singing before while composing their modern verse.

So next time you queue playlists kindling motivation, cushion heartaches or dance celebrating identity - remember legendary lineage of musical messaging powering seminal soundtrack for envisioning then manifesting revolution. LGBTQ+ musicians unravel isolation by broadcasting inner world echoed universally. Their rhythmic amplification carries once muffled stories to loudest stages until finally heard then immortalized echoing inspiration beyond limits of mortal words.

Curating Your Empowering Pride Playlist

Music unlocks profound emotional power during pivotal seasons of self-discovery and pride. Curating personalized playlists allows purposefully harnessing melodic medicine lifting hearts when challenges arise or celebrations merit soundtrack. Strategize song selections speaking solidarity to your story among diverse genres echoing varied voices. Let these suggestions showcase breadth across culture and eras kindling connection. Queue up then press play unleashing inspiration!

Mirrors Reflecting Back Self-Recognition

"Born This Way" by Lady Gaga With bold pronouncements like "No matter gay, straight or bi, lesbian, transgender life / I'm on the right track, baby / I was born to survive" - Lady Gaga affirms embracing differences defiantly. Upbeat pride anthem inspires living fearlessly.

"Girls Like Girls" by Hayley Kiyoko
   Lesbian musician Hayley Kiyoko serenades with saucy lyrics highlighting pansexual attraction between women. Unapologetic pride song stresses freedom loving whoever feels right.

"I Want to Break Free" by Queen While not explicitly LGBTQ+ labeled, Queen's musical imaginings push gender fluidity boundaries even in 80's mainstream. Frenetic beats reinforce boldly reinventing identity.

Romance & Relationships

"My My My!" by Troye Sivan Rising young gay artist Troye Sivan sings giddy praises new relationship bliss. Catchy dance celebration conveys queer love's magical butterflies.

"If I Were Your Woman" by Gladys Knight Empowering slow jam highlights sensual feminine pursuit of another woman. Timeless storytelling portrays vulnerability and affection in wooing romantic interest.

"Make Me Feel" by Janelle Monae Genre-blending modern hit portrays flirtatious encounter between Monae and both male/female crushes. Bi pride colors slippery subject navigating fluid desire.

Reclaiming & Rallying

"I'm Coming Out" by Diana Ross Diana Ross makes bold statements around owning identity and self-love with lyrics "There's no benefit in hiding" and "I want the world to know / Got to let it show."

"We R Who We R" by Kesha Glittery dance defiance fuels standing ground as authentic self with "We don't care we don't care / We don't care what you think." Chant along chorus amplifies Pride chutzpah.

"A Change is Gonna Come" by Sam Cooke While released during 1960's civil rights era, Sam Cooke's gorgeous vocals promising hope and overcoming injustice resonates widely for marginalized struggles - including anticipating LGBT equality victories.

Gender Self-Determination

"If I Was Your Girl" by MUNA This tender track gives glimpse into transgender experience with "I just wanna love you, if you let me / I'll never betray you, I'll never hurt you." Sweet storyline conveys universal relationship vulnerabilities.

"Man, I Feel Like A Woman" by Shania Twain
   Twain flips gender stereotypes pronouncing feminine freedom in rollicking country song. Playful lyrics wink "The best thing about being a woman / Is the prerogative to have a little fun" while subverting conformity.

Intersecting Identities

"Brown Skin Girl" by Beyoncé Uplifting anthem celebrates beauty of brown and black girls. Refreshing affirmation conveys inheriting Throne as rightful Queens - important intersection with LGBTQ+ representations often defaulting white.

"Take Me As I Am" by Sinéad Harnett Sinéad Harnett soulfully sings navigating self-worth and dating while black lesbian. Stirring vulnerability bridges multiple marginalized identities with wider resonance.

"Two Birds" by Regina Spektor Quirky ballad uses bird metaphor to explore reconciling Russian heritage with lesbian identity. Unique framing spotlights reconciling familial roots and culture with personal truths.

Defiant Hope & Healing

"Rainbow" by Kacey Musgraves Aching yet reassuring ballad conveys lingering post-trauma isolation with "storm is finally passing on" optimism. Musgraves wrote the song as message for marginalized youth envisioning better tomorrow.

"Fighter" by Christina Aguilera

Aguilera famously overcame abusive early career marketing reinventing stronger image and sound. Anthemic lyrics like "After all you put me through, / You'd think I'd despise you / But in the end, I wanna thank you" signal reclaiming power.

Intergenerational Classics

"Believe" by Cher Ageless gay icon Cher delivers fantastically autotuned club thumper about persisting through rocky romance. Timeless diva encourages resilience despite heartaches.

"Dancing Queen" by ABBA Joyously kitschy ode extols self-celebration command to dance, dance! Escapist lyrics salute "having the time of your life" fueling courage to live fabulously without apology.

Now equipped with starter set mix of beloved queer musical mirrors - let your personal pride playlist expand even louder. Venture discovering underground artists defying genres echoing your distinctive frequency. Let songs score this odyssey unveiling identity and owning destiny. Ultimately curate sounds kindling radical inspiration so your revolution rings harmonizing head high unapologetically!

Music as a Catalyst for Self-Discovery

Music's intimate lyrics, vulnerable vocal textures and rousing rhythms speak directly to the soul unlike any other artform. During turbulent eras of awakening inner truths yet fearing alienation, music becomes guiding light when all else darkens. The right songs trigger break-through clarity while offering reassuring mirrors that you walk not alone.

Take Ricardo, who grew up the only Latino student in his small midwestern hometown. While sensing attraction toward other boys, harsh slurs like "maricon" from relatives warned against expressing effeminate behaviors that might out himself. Lacking LGBTQ+ role models in isolated community complicated self-understanding amidst cultural pressures to perform masculinity and provide grandchildren someday.

In college Ricardo first discovered indie singer Mxmtoon, who proudly identifies as queer Asian American, bravely broadcasting messages embracing mental health struggles and nonconformity journeys. Hearing specific details like wishing "my mom would call me by my own name" regarding gender transition echoed Ricardo's swelling doubts whether family could ever truly know or support emerging identity. He clung lyrics promising "I know one day I won't have to hide" while waiting his own time feel safe externally conveying internal truths.

Brooklyn MC Young M.A's brazen lyrics proudly spotlighting her female masculinity and attraction toward women also resonated with Ricardo's layered intersectional exploration. Seeing butch lesbian woman of color boldly celebrate both identities - gender expansive and culturally rooted - fostered reconciling his initial perceptions of identities inherently conflicting. Slowly shame dissolved opening capacity envisioning integrating layered aspects of Latino queer himself.

Escaping Darkness Through Music

Josefina Vega recalls a traumatic queer childhood under Chile's Pinochet dictatorship absorbing murderous homophobia and violent repression against political activism. Burying her own awakening bisexuality to survive, she endured addiction and isolation trying to outrun identity supposedly too dangerous if discovered.

However 70's protest singer Victor Jara's pierce-your-spirit lyrics became lifeline resisting erasure. As queer icon Jara demanded through bold guitar chords and poetic Spanish verse "we will go on being born, opening paths in struggle" - Josefina felt seen while kindling her own smoldering resilience. She eventually immigrated pursuing graduate studies exploring intersection of sexual, artistic and political identities - directly inspired from Jara's defiant artistry under ruthless regime.

Today as clinical therapist, Josefina frequently recommends clients exploring their identity create coming out playlists. Finding even one song capturing essence of buried emotions or vision for liberating future self helps blast through oppressive isolation. She believes curating soundtrack uniquely mirroring their journey fosters owning destiny.

The Language Music Provides When Words Fail

Before teenage transgender journey, Hazel couldn't pinpoint source of simmering gender dysphoria anxiety. Pronoun discomfort? Social roles? Physical change longing? Therapy dialogue struggled conveying shapeless distress.

Oddly enough, Hazel's breaking point struck amidst dad's classic rock phase blaring Creedence Clearwater Revival hit "Bad Moon

Rising" warning "there's a bad moon on the rise". Immediate wave nausea, vertigo nearly fainting overwhelmed painfully mirroring stirring femme identity with lyrics "I see trouble on the way" - understanding instinctively path ahead held untold struggles if dare reveal this inner "bad moon" self offending external expectations.

That guttural reaction cemented awareness no longer denying or rationalizing away. Music's meditative properties amplified tearful epiphany. Shortly after Hazel openly identified as trans woman. She carries special playlists now when words inadequately convey heart's ever-evolving inner frontier.

Music Builds Bridges Of Belonging

When music touches hearts, no longer "other" but suddenly familiar. Lyrics revealing shared secret struggles build bonds beyond assumed barriers. Sociopolitical messaging raises consciousness then rallies action. Who hears truth once muted now loudly sung cannot dismiss injustice rotting status quo's facade.

That gospel choir swell, driving bass line or violin crescendo stirs undeniable transcending space and time. Outpourings of marginalized prayer soaked into melodies echoes eternally as long as ears receive and amplify next choruses calling liberation. All waiting wings ready soar free if offered platform shine.

So listen close the rhythms echoing your unfolding story and channel courage facing frontiers new identity brings. For soundtracks scoring milestones of self-discovery carve footpaths where footing uncertain. Anthems kindle torches showing way. Your song sweetly sung lights horizon unveiling once unimaginable vistas of radical hope.

Conclusion: Your Personal Soundtrack to Self-Discovery

Music's intimate embrace speaks the language of soul - giving voice when words fall short. Melodic mirrors reveal our inner frontiers often obscured except through rhythm's codes communicated implicitly bypassing constraints of literal dictionaries.

Like oxygen to flame, the right songs awaken and amplify identity awakening already underway yet tentatively daring public proclamation. As pioneering LGBTQ+ artists spelled salvation softening suffering's blows for isolated outcasts and misfits - their poetic solidarity taught generations that living truth aloud connects rather isolates.

So in reviewing musician's tales kindling self-recognition then rallying collective uprising - one clearly witnesses music's sheer force fueling liberation movements protecting life itself. The personal rebels against death-dealing dominant norms by proclaiming "we're here, we're queer and embracing all that means!" Though battles continue rallying equity under the law and cultural inclusion - music makes space witnessing the human story's next courageous verse crafted from margins now centered.

Yes still today turbulent uncertainty stirs those questioning inner truths while fearing external fallout. Not all doors open instantly with simply sweet melody. However long echoing playlist of those singing before you drown detractor voices as identity awakens. Crank up and belt out when isolation attacks! Move knowing your song finds company.

I encourage expressly curating sounds tailored holding space wherever now planted on journey toward self-love and actualization. Seek melodies capturing essence and anticipation of the vision within now daring declaration. Let them score milestones as each wave crests then Crash rupturing limiting notions of who you must conform to appease.

The point isn't finding labels perfectly prescribed but rather illuminating ongoing awakening identity's multidimensional layers. Playlists evolve like we do. Celebrate full diversity of artists spotlighting varied voices and depictions among vast LGBTQ+ landscape. When ready wings expand, sounds lift in flight if given space soar.

Trust music's capacity cracking through fears barricading free expression. Own playlist proud as badge of honor for every outdated assumption defied and barrier crossed settling more wholly into skin once alien. With headphones hear marginalized musicians testify: though dangers exist and injustice persists, living whole is the boldest rebellion setting captured dreams and solidarity contagiously alight so all badge forward awakened.

Now long legacy lines up behind you - great ancestry choir cheering night toward dawn. Our echoes don't fade but only amplify summoning future freedom now bolder declared than generations prior dared fathom. Channel artists weaponizing words and rhythms consorting the long-view toward equity. Know your song sweetly sung stirs destiny!

Crank up playlist power anthem pulling pretense aside as Emergence Day arrives. Strike your bold chord. For when soul music meets world eager receiving long-hidden full expression - revolution has already begun. Our chorus now swells boundless. Listen loud declaring: we breathe free here fully belonging because I am exactly who I was born to be!

The next mesmerizing movement awaits your voice...press play and let's dance liberation unfolding never how oppression predicted. The world has not heard such freedom sounds before!

8

Flocking Together in Fabulousness

The Significance of Queer Friendships

Beyond fiery pride and righteous activism, at its heart the LGBTQ+ movement springs from remarkably ordinary source - the sustaining gift of human friendship. Within simple gestures of companionship and camaraderie blossom solidarity's first murmurs then explosive uprisings reversing tides of injustice. The story resides less in one leader's loud legacy but rather grassroots uncompromising love lifting entire communities toward long-denied liberties.

When dominant culture antagonizes difference prompting fragmentation, ostracization and internalized oppression - queer friendships model bold belonging that heals. Shared wisdom awake navigating identity awakenings carves pathways where none visible before. Echoed laughter eases burdens when even biological family relations strain under society's weighty norms. And in bonding together, once tentative voices strengthen into waves crashing walls that separate freedom's shore ahead.

So while rainbow waving pride parades appear primarily political spectacle - in truth they convene ritually recharging resilience tanks running on empty from battling institutional biases all year long. Reunions rejuvenate. Through simple acts of showing up for one another, visibility victors emerge not alone but gathered hand-in-hand.

Organizers emphasize friendship seeds all things, even liberation. Behind bold podium speeches lie intimate coaching conversations confirming potential first from within. Over honored elder's shoulders beam mentored youth honing skills to carry movements forward. Within hotel conference rooms, neighborhood bars and apartment dinner parties - strategic vision incubates then manifests policy and culture shifts protecting generations unborn.

Herein unveils chosen family's profound significance securing emotional and physical safety alternative structures lack. When crisis strikes systems not designed to nurture different identities - friends sustain each other preventing devastation. Gathered into intentional communities, outcasts eat, sleep, play choosing to walk together rather than wander lost unable quenching soul starvation mainstream denies exist.

So do not underestimate friendship's formidable force undergirding and advancing equity. At the heart of activism lies shared vulnerability and vision-driven hope etched through human hands holding tight. And there is no power greater than unconditional love awakening outcast's brightest belonging.

The Power of Queer Friendships

Navigating identity awakening and charting liberation's course requires resilient emotional muscles daily exercising vulnerability, courage and unconditional loving support. Space materializes testing unsteady new wings when trusted confidants walk alongside. LGBTQ+

friendships formed from shared experiences foster this soul sanctuary when other relationships strain under dominant norms.

Mirrors Reflecting Back Identity

In glimpsing personal complexities and insecurities mirrored through another's journey unraveling similar revelations around attraction benchmarks or gender alignments not conforming - burden of "otherness" lifts. Usually unspoken constructs exposing difference dissipate through friendship elevating essence of inner selves beyond surface identities.

As Asher, early transitioning non-binary youth, described, "My trans best friends just get me. We obsess together about the changes testosterone's working through body and mind, banter about crushes, hype each other up before doctor appointments or visiting families struggling our emergence. Away from others' eyes constantly questioning if I know myself, I feel certain."

Through unconditional reflection of each other's wholeness, certainty settles confidently inhabiting unfolding truths. Mirrors reinforce relying on internal wisdom above external skepticism.

Empathy Rooted in Lived Experience

Even closest open-minded allies cannot fully comprehend nuance walking LGBTQ+ path from formative identity imprints through later disclosure fallouts. Minority stress compounds through pervasive systems neither designed nor motivated accommodating difference.

However within queer friendship space no need explain significance behind gender euphoria high when properly gendered by strangers nor devastation struck when enduring misgendering malice. Pain poured out over yet another regional rights reversal or religious tirade lands receptive ears from those similarly immersed along society's edges. Being fully known and seen offers refuge.

As Nikki describes of Alok, their non-binary best friend, "I relax utterly around another queer person of color with activism roots like me. We are nameless, formless, fully spirit laughing loud. Between us exists this whole beautiful understanding of landscapes we commonly traverse yet remains mysterious overseas needing constant translation adapting others' norms." Through shared lens unique vistas of hope make sense.

Chosen Family Security

LGBTQ+ elders emphasize wisdom - home is where they have to take you in. When existing family structures fail nurturing wholeness emerging through identity shift, responsibility falls choosing environments that embrace your full self. However without role models or resources familiarity mainstream inherits, envisioning certainly less manifesting alternative "families" appears utterly daunting.

Alishya expresses, "Everything changed once queer friends brought me into their radical family activating my passions. We pooled money securing communal housing when individual paychecks insecurely cover rent in expensive city. There emotional safety nets catch unpredictable setbacks life throws defending layered identities. While biological families mean well but miss marks understanding, chosen families secure my whole being."

Research consistently demonstrates LGBTQ+ individuals embedded among affirming communities Reporting significantly higher self-esteem, life satisfaction and resilience managing minority stressors - thanks inheriting families of choice able consistently nurture the need for mirroring, understanding and belonging required thriving. Ties binding deeper than water or blood but rather soul and vision.

Shared Paths Carving Future Footsteps

So in these divided times, recall nothing erodes illusion of "otherness" quite like human stories kindling camaraderie. Revolutionary concepts need testing grounds germinating from skin hunger to secure attachment. Political applications emerge later only secondary to individuals' compassion awakening. Empathy extends first through unspoken kindness between people while erecting wings upward lifting justice higher.

There is no doubt - friendships plant seeds of equitable society envisioning concerns of one intrinsically bound to liberation of all. When souls truly see, hear and know one another - false separations dissolve upon touch. Take courage and see beyond strangers to counterparts walking shared terrain. Here await friends already recognizing your arrival's significance joining the prophetic momentum resisting alone no more.

Anecdotes of Meaningful Connections

Behind every watershed political victory, before each orchestra's first harmonizing swell or any towering artistic legacy left behind - simple human stories unfold navigating significance of identity and life's meaning stitched by bonds of friendship. Within intimate vulnerability and shared resonance of these ordinary moments blossoming between lives, the extraordinary uprising manifests one courageous reach toward authentic living inspires another.

Friends as Family Through Life's Seasons

When Jose was suddenly kicked out from Catholic parents home having accidentally outed gay identity, homeless desperation magnified trauma. Offering shelter during devastating limbo before stable housing and work secured, Jose's childhood friend Gabby refused letting tearful 2am phone call go unanswered. Her spare bedroom welcomed immediate refuge from external storm. Inside jokes over bowls of takeout Chinese food reconnected severed sense safety during weeks struggling nightmares about uncertain future.

Though personally straight, Gabby insisted Jose stay helping navigate legal resources, counseling options and career mentor referrals until confidently standing independently again. When holiday isolation stung seeing happy families celebrating on social media, Gabby showed up as surrogate sibling celebrating "Friendsgiving" remembering true family never disowns. Decades later, Veteran community organizers Jose and Gabby maintain fierce kinship mentoring next generations LGBTQ+ leadership. Gabby beams, "In bare times unveiled humanity's true face. Hardship clarified life's meaning is showing up through little ways and big - no matter what hangs balance."

Impacting Young Lives

As transgender teacher navigating professional constraints around identity disclosure, instructing High Schoolers through awkward adolescence Steven connected quick-witted student Permission to start Gender Sexuality Alliance chapter. Brainstorming event programming together like queer author readings, collaborating on curriculum integrating positive LGBTQ+ historical figures and even chaperoning school dances to prevent discriminatory incidents cultivated closeness.

Steven reflects "Angela appeared leader within student body, but privately confided paralyzing fears social life plummeting if came out lesbian. My mentoring through early stages self-acceptance until confidently applying out-of-state queer friendly college made all the bureaucracy red tape seem worth enduring. I understood isolation facing journey inward without visible role models outward mirroring unfolding truths. Guiding Angela toward self-love and paths embracing identity felt sacred trust."

Years forward attending Angela's law school graduation Steven wept seeing confident young woman now advocating justice. Pride shone realizing planted seeds assuming responsibility for next generation's growth to fruit sweeter world ahead.

Building Shared Destiny of Equitable Society

College ethnically displaced Sylvester but bright spirit attracted queer exchange student crew smiling unexpected belonging during disorienting transition. Senior classman Derek welcomed newcomer's conversational wit into lively Thursday sushi dinner banter nights.

Academically gifted Derek tutored Sylvester navigating scholarship applications fortifying dreams but meager civil engineering budget living overseas alone never afforded. Sleeping spare room Derek's off-campus apartment once monthly heated water pipe floods forced moving rescued housing nightmare. Friendship transcended circumstance.

What began as cheerful company among outsiders in foreign university manifested lifelong colleague bond across countries today. Having secured advanced engineering degrees and positions back governing developing nations infrastructure, their international friendship now collaborates consulting projects improving living standards together imagining policies benefiting all people regardless of identity. Sylvester now pays forward Derek's gift welcoming each confused student knocking fateful door.

Blossoming Where Life Plants

And so unfolds the quiet legacy of love rising simple human experience yet eroding barricades once deemed indestructible. When hearts hang tethered by shared essence deeper than surface labels, hope whispers gently but persistently watering identity seeds until most vibrant unimagined blooms erupt boldly from unassuming soil. All daring live the truth as inner light reveals expands possibility enough for outstretched hands clasp comforting night toward dawn. Stay close and witness coming liberation. Destiny awaits downstream for those awakening banks no longer isolating but that together hold the course.

Cultivating and Nurturing Relationships

While shared identity awakening holds innate bonding power, actively nurturing connection roots friendships fortifying years beyond initial resonance. Apply wisdom securing relationships thriving long-term. Where energy flows generously without tallying give-receive balances, bonds deepen weaving lives strength together.

Communication Builds Trust

Ensure communicating clearly, honestly and compassionately remains priority. Schedule recurring check-ins as lives progress navigating diverse opportunities and challenges that may strain connecting. Voice appreciations, insecurities, confusion or hurts soon arising before simmering resentment at mismatched needs poisons mutual understanding.

Remember perceptions wonderfully complex and customizable. Ask clarifying questions rather assume blanket intentions. Welcome discussing tensions noticing projection tendencies assuming others' motives mirroring your own. Lead extending patience or forgiveness modeled seeking first understanding over reactively judging.

Cultivate self-awareness managing emotional triggers from past relational wounds that close your heart too quickly when relationships hit inevitable rough patches needing nurturing most. Consider embracing couples counseling exploring communication tools strengthening bonds beyond surface attraction into intimate lasting partnership.

Shared Activities Deepen Closeness

Of course enjoy and make time celebrating life's major milestones marking growth like new jobs, creative projects unfolding or healing intergenerational family wounds. But also plant seeds growing connection through smaller consistent rituals commemorating friendship as pillar providing ballast when greater storms arise.

Organize weekly community dinner potlucks with rotating hosts or movie viewing parties discussing themes relatable to your journey. Volunteer mutually meaningful cause lifting marginalized voices. Start two person book club or attend workshops fostering personal development. Shared activities infuse spiritual nourishment into regular routines preventing isolation stagnating relationships otherwise distracted modern life.

Chosen Family RequiresIntentionality

While some LBGTQ+ individuals report families of origin lovingly embracing identity shifts, realities often prove complicated. When external support structures collapse, necessity demands proactively engineering "families of choice" providing alternative emotional/practical foundations securing safety needs going unmet.

Research chosen families intentionally rather desperately reacting crisis. Seek wise mentors noticing knowledge gaps needing patient guidance unpacking internalized shame or strategic skill-building navigating career barriers faced being out. Show up participating local queer organizations or befriend fellow activists fighting shared social justice causes lifting oppressed communities. Join recreational leagues building fun comradery around hobbies breeding joyful existence.

Yes situating one's whole self securely within chosen family oasis requires stretching beyond comfort zones taking relational risks many avoid. However injecting vulnerability asking for and extending care lays rewarding groundwork forging ties overtaking traditional knots when ecology of home culture fails nourishing authentic being. Plant seeds that in time interlace roots stabilizing fresh terrain where you and loved ones blossom freely together.

Flocking Together in Your Journey

In reviewing power woven through strands of queer friendship, clearly no courageous victory claimed nor height reached alone but rather banding together as comrades shouldering unfolding voyage side-by-side. When wings grow weary or gales threaten knocking off course, flock lifts secure in communal migrations mapping destiny beyond limitations feared insurmountable venturing solo. What friendship nurtures is faith knowing your hand held when uncertainty surroundings darkens the visible way ahead.

So as you chart next legs exploring identity or charting life purpose amplified once barriers limiting free expression begin dissolving, I implore investing caring community tucked under arm for whatever awaits around destiny's corner. For while media flashes lone pioneers bravely resisting convention to manifest radically authentic living - behind curtain truth reveals years, often decades spent stumbling uncertain early trails before standing confidently visible later. Only through consistent compassion keeping company did they transform inner truths into bold living testaments advancing inclusive culture.

Yes finding such kindred spirits may require looking beyond surface introductions and familiar signposts commonality claims. But where essence resonates no matter packaging differently conveyed, begin practicing vulnerability muscles that interweave fulfilling bonds holding space should greater injury strike. Start conversing more courageously. Extend generosity without knowing guaranteed reciprocal return but modeling dignity for its own sake. Lean closer discerning glimmers familiarity kindling though expressions walk varied.

Life continually unfolds growth opportunities awakening next self not previously reflecting back from mirrors society holds. Revelations once devastating and isolating turn joyful when trusted allies amplify witnessing each phase passing through death into daring rebirth. Then dried tears give way to laughter. Identity crises cede to celebrations of essence and gifts waiting discovered once masks fall away. Fierce compassion answer unrestrained, for when wings expand contracted conditional love suffocates full spectral emergence awaiting flight beyond fears we all carry when walking alone.

I assure companionship abounds as friendship models life's true meaning is showing up through little ways and big - no matter what hangs balance. When nobody gets left behind to wander lost invisible, destiny quickens pace from dream toward reality lived boldly proud each unique yet united contribution honoring the grander migrations ahead. We all have more still to learn and more still to love.

So boldly declare "As I am, I fly high". Then grasp hand not far recognizable as co-sojourner charting course less traveled. Companions surface as this age-old story writes next chapter raised from margins now pierced mainstream hearing first cries righteously declaring "we breathe proud and free here as one people indivisible!" Listen close and you will discern the chorus awaiting your strand melodically woven in the greater tapestry conveying this destiny forward unleashed completely. Let friends surround lifting loneliness as wings expand toward liberation sky no longer limited but boundless.

9

Dance Like Nobody's Watching

The Transformative Power of Dance

Among the marvelous diversity of art forms, dance uniquely traverses boundaries connecting human souls through undeniably universal languages transcending spoken word's limitations. Graceful yet primal gestures, rhythm's infectious pulse driving hearts to embody joy pulsing alive, sensual movement uninhibited by convention's constraints - here swells immediate communion often elusive semantic attempts directly conveying life's depth.

For whether witnessing stories staged purposefully through choreographed leaps and lifts, or spontaneously whirling together unrehearsed as festive music spontaneously moves the spirit - dancing emerges communal cauldron seamlessly melding individual expression into powerful shared experience. Forward bursts truth typically buried under reflexive social manners and polite conformity. Dance's direct vocabulary speaks soul depths beyond where language left wanting.

And from these flowing wellsprings of momentary liberation springs dancing's transformative promise unleashing fuller liberation ahead. Within compelling motion stirs longings for unhinging from fears too often holding identity and voice hostage. As bodies sway unrestrained no longer self-conscious witnessing similarly engaged neighbors, hearts lift observing humanity's splendid spectrum on display hearts equally beating the drum's summoning toward unity.

For LGBTQ+ people historically pushed margins by cultural exclusion, gatherings spinning wild freedom on dance floors tastes the first inklings of a more just world glimpsed through temporary windows music opens. Even before courage consolidates confronting societal barriers barricading authentic living, imaginative space materializes in dancing breathlessly through what rapturous existence awaiting past constricting norms broken. The dance floor models fervent hope alighting destiny ahead.

So powerful proves this intuitive inner knowing through dancing's ephemeral magic that dance emerges recurring ritual through eras advancing LGBTQ+ culture toward full inclusion. From underground balls fiercely competing victorious self-expression, to festive Pride events unifying calls for awareness and solidarity to Hollywood's screen spotlighting dazzling queer artistry for mass consumption - dance propels witnessing outcast's visible belonging now refusing retreat. The revolution broadcasts through songs bodies sing exultant and unbound exactly as created: worthy divine beauty commanding respect and honor by sheer human right.

Dance stands poised shouting ongoing invitations to live freely bold above unjust norms once wielding weapons wordless but mighty breaking internal chains binding fluid identity. Surrounding sound waves clear wide planes once deemed impossible lifting all up celebrating shared magnificence when fear flees melodies opening hearts. Ready feet...music begins and with it liberation's next expansive wave unfolds through rhythms felt truly seeded souls now flowering individual yet undeniably and beautifully one.

The Emotional Liberation of Dance

Dance's irresistible allure transcends entertaining artform but rather channels intuit heart's yearnings through motion's catharsis. When rhythms stir and bodies respond instinctively flowing where beats lead detached constraints self-consciousness imposes, emotion finds freeing embodiment expression. Movements unlock feelings and experiences sometimes too complex conveyed words bound rigid dictionaries. Through dance liberation quakes foundations clinging constrictive conventions slowly now giving way.

Releasing Suppressed Emotions

Tapping kinetic vocabulary conveying what inner wells struggle containing, dance provides portal releasing suppressed emotional burdens easier stored tense muscles and anxiously spinning thoughts than honestly acknowledged. Gathering denied feelings once dangerously explosive, dance alchemizes intensity into creative power athletically channeled. No longer weapon but wonderment reclaiming agency on identity terms.

Brooklyn-based queer Latinx therapist Dr. Marta Moreno recognizes referring clients explore movement practices like contact improvisation, ecstatic dance, 5Rhythms or Authentic Movement often "unlocks energetic armoring" where traumatic memory lodged now gently massaged through welcoming immersion sensory experiencing. Finding home calmly inhabiting skin and breath grants deeper reflection insight once overwhelm flooded clarity. Through dancing distress… healing begins.

Channeling Joy

But not only pain finds flowing outlet freed through movement's mystery. Equally dance waves joy rippling delightful channels delight's swell no longer contained when rhythm rocks exultant celebration this gift called living. Feel goodness ground-up boots stomping grateful ability carry bodies navigating life's complex terrain. Holler hallelujahs hips jubilantly transverse no longer chained but liberated. Dance dares literally leap entitlement embodying delight.

Research increasingly confirms benefits generating positive emotions facilitates more flexible mindset and creative outlook expanding life possibilities over tunnel vision dwelling fear or anger evoke. Dance rouses whole being - heart, mind, body and spirit - toward awakening birthright happiness too often obscured under survivalist lens modernity narrows. Letting loose through music births courage carrying fuller identity joyfully as slow shuffle begins backsliding heavy emotions once inevitable managing marginalization's realities. Bliss bubbles moving meditation lifting higher.

Owning Voice and Identity

Furthermore dance strengthens emergent identity by seizing bold platform displaying self-definition unapologetically, unseen muted wallflower shying spotlights. When bodies unabashed occupy space, inner light beams brighter no longer questions cowering "Who am I to…" but rather declares "Here I am!" willing vulnerability. Confidence accrues stepping powerfully purposeful to rhythms aligned soul's signature beat.

Try blasting anthems stoking conviction, don sacred apparel crowning fullest self-concept then move intuitively through rooms no longer corner hiding but center stage unmuted spectacle. Through dancing identity loudly emerge someone once hesitant now proudly commanding full attention, respect and celebration by sheer audacious presence. Bold movement mocks limitations once monopolizing identity bandwidth. Make space and let authentic entity erupt.

Connecting with Your Body Through Dance

Beyond emotional catharsis, dance fosters deeper embodiment appreciating physical form as vessel central living earthly existence. When disconnected mind harshly judges natural shapes bodies inhabit, insecurity and distress compounds identity awakening already turbulent waters. However redirected loving attention through movement mends splits mind/body into integrated celebration precisely unique incarnation manifested this life for some destiny ahead.

Reuniting with Body's Wisdom

Consider closing eyes begin scanning conscious awareness throughout entire body noticing where breath flows easily or tension clings. Send accepting presence into sensation world right below your neck reconciling perhaps years neglecting somatics beneath intellectual fixation. As dancers say "stand in your skin" inhabiting this fantastically complex coordinating organism far beyond ornamental objectifications. What undulating feelings or textures reveal here now if listening within?

Many somatic movement schools aim heal splits modern life creates externally directed productivity compulsions far outpacing caring inner home facilitating being before doing. Notice what creative impulses guide hips, spine and shoulders when music plays left undissected critical thoughts? Through returning body and attending innate sensory brilliance already operating independently cognitive control, reclaim authority joyfully steering life rhythms soulfully aligned.

Building Body Attunement

Beyond passive listening body's subtle inner stirrings, actively engage practices reuniting with full embodied awareness. Dance/movement therapy provides guided self-exploration via incremental prompts inviting non-judgmental investigation reaction physicality when responding various directed invitations. Noticing without analysis builds finer attunement mind/body fuller expression unconstrained. Consider searching local practitioner or online trainings engaging guided session from trained facilitators.

Additionally local studios offering conscious dance and ecstatic movement provide space playfully encountering physical listening as supportive community gathers sharing healing intentions. When surrounded fellow explorers similarly seeking liberate identities once confined narrow social constructs, creativity awakens interplay vibrant energy flowing room center together yet distinct. Be moved, laugh and maybe even cry together in motion rediscovering birthright freedom loving form you inhabit.

For LGBTQ+ community struggling compounded stigma internalized judging appearances somehow invalid, somatic arts powerfully reconnect human substance behind politicized bodies rendered battleground legislation seeking control. Reclaim authority you are perfectly created magnificent complex creature spirit interwoven. This body and being delivered already equipped handling life's journeys ahead. As dancer Martha Graham said "the body never lies" …so ask yours today where truth awaits next steps ahead aligned.

Dancing in Different Spaces

Dance's liberating power flows anywhere creative courage moves one stepping beyond limiting constructs towards authentic identity expression. While professional venues platform polished performances, equally sacred dances stir club corners, kitchen tiles or forest groves once rhythm stirs conviction proclaiming untamed spirit within rising bold.

Personal Spaces

Consider candid moments no audience but your own critical presence bears witness shedding inhibitions anyway. Alone where none judge, turn music setting soul ablaze then permit limbs and lyrics proclaim suppressed passions aloud. Be foolish, be scared, be unconcerned cradling whatever arises non-judgmentally. Then Channel through movement prayers your waking life may otherwise resist manifesting in daylight beyond internal realms.

Dance unbound in bedrooms and bathrooms that knew past versions of self before growing toward current fuller identity. Allow environments holding previous painful memories to be exorcised demons haunting freedom with unreserved movement sanctifying every corner with vivid aliveness no longer haunting pain projected these walls back. Make space for integrating identity facets long segregated different locations… dance truth through halls until outlives shame once silencing thriving expression.

Public Dance Floors

While personal dance catharsis heals inner fragmentation, collective dance floors seed boldest vision public spaces fostering unity through diversity's vivid tapestry jointly feeling indivisible rhythmic heartbeat. Together pulse conjures upwellings of courage and solidarity that back outside club doors hardy withstand mainstream indifference continuing misunderstanding LGBTQ+ lives. But illuminated rooms resonating with destigmatizing delight model microcosm of inclusive world possible.

Research affirms positive emotions' contagion and group flow states generating shared meaning elevating individuals thus communities culminating coordinated social change. Dance floor joking and soulful lyrical exchanges build bonds above passing pleasantry. Strangers become neighbors when jointly stepping toward destiny's steady beat. Here lies vision's ignition awaits translating insight into action beyond momentary escape social alienation that marginalized identities face entering outside unforgiving norms.

So dance unabashed under glittering lights beside those witnessing intimate processes unfolding storied journeys toward empowered identity integration. And let boldness reverberate wider waves understanding complexity only possible through courageously dancing vulnerable edges aloud together.

Building Inclusive Dance Communities

Recognize that for LGBTQ+ individuals facing compounded marginalization like people of color, those physically disabled or crossing many spectrums identities - communal dance floors provoke added social anxieties lacking proper safety cues that privilege never registers. Ensure DJs foster welcoming atmospheres for diversity through pronouncing preferred pronouns, avoiding explicit language and stating no tolerance harassment plus reporting procedures if occurs. Sober companions greatly support vulnerable friends navigating nightlife.

Educate bouncers handle expressions gender fluidity with respect when confirming identity. Specify accessibility preferences venues when possible assuring needed accommodations get provided through wide aisles wheelchairs plus elevated stages visible short statured. Model patience graceful inclusive guidance supporting all learning dancefloor etiquette.

When witnessing tension arise surrounding diversity expressions call higher ground respecting all share the dancefloor seeking pleasure principles peace, love, unity and having fun! Together ensure this liberating space expands from within each heart so outer solidarity reflects soon inevitable result. The dance continues as destiny's feet step sure steady drumbeat bending arch justice until all arrive shores once deemed impossible fate beyond reach.

Embrace the Dance of Self-Expression

In reviewing dance's resplendent power animating stuck places within and channeling voices once silenced by conformity's vice grip - clearly much more at play than merely entertaining artform but rather liberating instrument for reclaiming identity's creative fire. Through rhythms stirring surrender beyond mental controls, revelation takes form unfolding untethered personal and collective destiny waiting wings spread.

I assure however faltering first steps, the dance inevitably takes over when truly surrendered. For even few moments sincerely dropping limiting notions correct aesthetic forms and simply feeling way through music's medicine...ancient wisdom stirs remembering original birthright unobstructed belonging. Here emerge first tastes beckoning the grand unfolding ahead.

So dare ask where movement intuitively pulls longing expression too complex or dangerous express vulnerable sharing by daylight? Then dance prayer with unconcern for critical gaze that shrivels soul gifts nurtured dark before ripened prepared facing external elements. Protect these tender stirrings from rational dismissal quick judging surreal sensations initially beyond describable form.

Start subtly swaying in kitchen humming favorite song once publicly danced full out. Loosen limbs lifted by nostalgic score remembering how loafing laughter detached worrisome weights real world pinned down. In coy hallways shuffle hope awaiting grander ballrooms ahead. For when courage first channels truth through motion's poetry - identity long distorted finds clarity claimed bold once fear screams silenced by rhythmic revelation. We each hold far more magnificent beauty and creative force than external norms conditioned believing. Dance dare unlock the radical revolution arising from within.

Twirl unscripted adventures awaiting known and unknown both. Sometimes solo flights fancy private escapades turn public spectacle displaying gifts once closeted as social norms evolve more inclusive seeing. Or gather tribe testing declarations of unapologetic authentic identity together on floors consecrated by generations pioneering self-disclosure under hostile ignorance. For where lovers lounge rhythm recovered, revolutions found clearing!

I assure however clumsy carriage carries your journey now, more possible than logic limits. But do tap patience discovering movement vocabulary conveying layered complexities identity unfolding. There are no wrong steps, just the next bold chance channeling most genuine full spectrum self awaiting performance once conventions constraining identity fade irrelevant. Keep dancing!

Soon enough momentum builds inner tides strengthens while structures obstructing fluid expression give way. Identity integrated finds elder wise within carrying home this temporary body beyond lifetime's curtain call. Rhythms pulse eternal. Each corded constellation composed diversity frees next adventurous steps ahead. Together dance impossible gauging dreams into being!

So throw open soul doors further feel that fierce liberating fire rhythm reawakens. Let poetry pierce through motions what resigns lifeless hiding numbed from unforgiving social temerity blind conformity breeds. Shake awake! Now 1..2...3... dance truest you into world eagerly awaiting your brightest boldest awakened, activated and aligned!

10

Redefining Success in a Spectrum of Colors

Rethinking Success in the LGBTQ+ Spectrum

What does it mean to be successful? Society often holds up fame, fortune, power, and material possessions as the pinnacle of achievement. However, when we look within marginalized communities, including the LGBTQ+ spectrum, traditional markers of success rarely tell the whole story.

Within queer spaces, theJourney to self-acceptance and community belonging often transforms one's perspective on what constitutes a life well-lived. External validation through money, status, or conformity to societal standards loses relevance compared to inner fulfillment, personal growth, and connection to others with shared experiences. The ability to live as one's authentic self becomes success in its purest form.

However, this is not meant to diminish the very real systemic barriers and discrimination that make traditional success difficult for LGBTQ+ people to obtain. Rather, it spotlights the need to challenge narrow definitions of success and acknowledge that people across the gender and sexuality spectrum define thriving life paths in diverse ways

The Life Stories Behind the Letters

Behind the LGBTQ+ initialism stand colorful stories of resilience, self-discovery, and pride. Lesbians, gays, bisexuals, transgender people, queer/questioning individuals, and other non-heteronormative identities reflect a beautifully complex community. However, some letters have traditionally dominated the conversation more than others.

For example, trans people and issues often get relegated to the sidelines in mainstream society and even within LGBTQ+ spaces. The unique challenges faced by trans folks, including gender dysphoria, discrimination, violence, and lack of legal protections in healthcare, housing, and employment, impact definitions of success and ability to meet basic needs. Simply surviving and carving out any measure of fulfillment becomes its own success.

Likewise, for intersex people born with variations in physical sex characteristics, early non-consensual surgical interventions focused on "normalizing" anatomy rather than wellbeing shape life's journey from the start. Healing physically and emotionally to embrace one's whole self offers an alternate form of achievement.

Furthermore, asexual, aromantic, non-binary, and more identities frequently left out of the acronym fight similar battles for visibility, understanding, and control over one's destiny. Creating inclusive community support networks to nurture self-love reframes the goals.

For LGBTQ+ seniors, the climb was especially steep, as many endured decades of secrecy and denial of civil rights during less accepting times. For youth just discovering and questioning identity in a rapidly changing cultural landscape, different trials emerge. Generational divides reveal contrasting vantage points.

In the end, the letters stand not just for identities but for the steps individuals take to write their own stories – often filled with setbacks and triumphs – toward some version of self-defined success.

Queering the Mainstream Idea of Success

Take a mental snapshot of a "successful person." What springs to mind?

Adjectives like wealthy, attractive, popular and accomplished likely dominate, with markers like a fancy house, nice car, trophy spouse, big promotion, and professional prestige. But this archetype narrowly reflects cisgender, heterosexual, and gender-conforming experiences.

Now tear up that photo. Crumple it up tight and toss it straight into the recycling bin marked "societal conditioning."

Let's get creative and colorful with our visualization of success expressed across the entirety of LGBTQ+ spaces. Start with a blank canvas, ready to be filled with vibrant visions of authentic lives well-lived.

Maybe the image takes shape as someone comfortably wearing long hair, make-up, dresses, and heels for the first time, finally embracing their feminine gender identity after years of denial. Or it's a lesbian couple blissfully dancing at their beach wedding, never imagining as closeted teens that they could one day legally marry. Perhaps it's a proud parent beaming at their child's school talent show, grateful the open-minded school warmly welcomes their gender-creative kid who likes dressing up in feather boas.

Success through a LGBTQ+ positive lens also sparkles in small moments: the rush of excitement chatting online with a queer pen pal across the globe who "just gets it," the swell of feeling at home in an LGBTQ+ welcoming spiritual community, the joy of finding a favorite book character or TV hero with whom one deeply identifies. It pulses in LGBTQ+-owned businesses bringing queer joy, advocacy and economic mobility to communities long bereft of inclusive spaces.

Infinite Perspectives Shape Success

Of course, no singular narrative defines the LGBTQ+ experience, as it crosses an unlimited spectrum of identities, personalities, upbringings, cultures, eras and communities. Ultimately, success follows no formula.

A transgender activist might measure it through expanded legal protections, awareness building, or client caseload victories. For a young bisexual still discovering identity, success may mean reconciling faith and sexuality through an affirming theology class. An asexual committed partnership could redefine coupled bliss by rejecting society's emphasis on sex. A rising non-binary performer might view packed shows and fans connecting with their message as professional actualization.

Even failure gets reassessed under a queer lens. Setbacks along the winding road to self-understanding often build resilience and catalyze growth. Discrimination can fertilize righteous anger and drives for change. Internalized negativity and shame may spark greater self-love through undoing past hurt.

What traditional metrics overlook are the intangible triumphs: hope sparked through authentic representation, courage built through visibility boosting community bonds, confidence uncovered by resisting conformity.

Fulfillment, Understanding and Belonging

So let's challenge ourselves to expand visions of fruitful lives beyond society's narrow take. Diverse LGBTQ+ experiences bring richness and insight to illuminate blind spots. The letters LGBTQ encompass endless stories, perspectives and paths waiting to be heard, shared, and uplifted.

By embracing authentic personal definitions of success, we can combat the destructive messaging that marginalizes those who color outside conformist lines. We can run joyfully into our multifaceted future, without fear that being our true selves will make us somehow "less than" in realizing our dreams.

Underneath all the labels lives the universal human needs for self-understanding, belonging and purpose. By recasting societal yardsticks for achievement, LGBTQ+ spaces model how to cultivate our growth in our own shapes – bending in beautiful ways some may call crooked but we call glorious.

Unpacking Societal Expectations and Labels

We live in a world obsessed with norms. From the standardized tests that track academic progress to the binary gender checkboxes everywhere we turn, society narrowly defines what counts as "normal" and applies pressure to conform. For LGBTQ+ people, these norms exclude the natural diversity of gender and sexuality that has always existed. Expectations rooted in mainstream societal values make it hard for queer folks to chart their own definitions of success.

Heteronormativity and cisnormativity – the assumption that heterosexuality and cisgender identity (identifying with one's sex assigned at birth) constitute normal – permeate cultural messages. These biases privilege straight and cis experiences as ideal while branding LGBTQ+ lives as abnormal, unnatural, even immoral deviations from the prescribed path.

Life Inside the "Closet of Heteronormativity"

Think of society's imposing norms around sexuality and gender as a closet that no one exactly chooses to enter. From birth, mainstream social messaging quietly closes the door, making coming out a necessary journey whether one ultimately identifies as LGBTQ+ or not. We all must first shed limiting assumptions before embracing unique truths about ourselves.

What does that invisibility inside the closet of heteronormativity feel like across LGBTQ+ spaces?

- For closeted LGBTQ+ youth, it often means torment, confusion and danger without support systems. Bullied queer kids show higher risks of self-harm, family rejection, homelessness, school dropout, and suicide when the only visible options seem unacceptable. Success lies not in some distant achievement but in making it safely through each day.
- For transgender individuals, walking in a society that refuses to see diverse gender identities creates a suffocating distortion between outer perception and inner truth. Fighting to emerge as oneself despite risks takes courageous defiance.
- Bisexual people in different-sex relationships disappear behind society's binary gay or straight assumption. Constant coming out becomes exhausting lip service for basic visibility.
- Non-binary and gender non-conforming people scrape to find fitting words to describe bodies and experiences that society tries to squash into Woman/Man boxes. Crafting new language opens up narrow perceptions.

Escaping the closet that hides LGBTQ+ reality takes prying open society's door for all of us. Gaining basic understanding, legal rights and safety precedes defining well-rounded success.

Measuring Up on Society's Scales

Picture the iconic symbol of justice – the Roman goddess Justitia blindfolded and balancing her scales. Except when judging LGBTQ+ lives, society peeks out from behind that blindfold, adding biased weights to tip the scales.

Queer folks must prove extra worth to reach equal footing, overcoming distorted perceptions. Do you play straight enough? Align expectations based on your assigned sex? Uphold respectable morals? Benefit the mainstream? Only then does the scale concede balance.

What warped weights do people across LGBTQ spaces confront?

- For gay men, it often means meeting masculine ideals – strong, stoic, successful, sexually potent with mainstream attractiveness. Feminine, flamboyant, or gender non-conforming gay men tilt off balance. Bisexual men called confused or greedy for not picking a side teeter on the edge.
- Lesbians backload ambition, intelligence and responsibility to stabilize gender non-conformity. Lipstick feminine ideals or unrealistic coupledom put idealized weights on the one side. Sexualized exoticization or predatory assumptions burden the other.
- For trans people, their entire right to exist as their authentic selves gets called into question. Requirements to medically transition or "pass" convincingly challenge those unable or unwilling to meet cisnormative expectations. Non-binary identities altogether fall through society's scales unmeasured.
- Asexual and aromantic people, who feel little or no sexual/romantic attraction, buck expectations of universal desire and

coupling. They challenge norms by showing life fulfillment with less conventional relationship forms or without any partner at all.

Queer people grow exhausted trying to measure up in systems rigged against them. But slowly, society's unjust scales lose credibility and relevance. Self-acceptance tips the balance inward, questioning the validity of outside reviewers determining queer folks' worth at all.

Identity Above Expectations

While societal biases stack the odds, amazing LGBTQ+ successes emerge when individuals walk their own paths. queer joy and resilience resists confinement.

Take iconic transgender actress Laverne Cox. Her 2014 Time magazine cover declaring the "transgender tipping point" shattered expectations on magazine racks nationwide. Or genderfluid Jaden Smith boldly wearing dresses to combat toxic masculinity. Trailblazers make once unimaginable visibility seem effortless through authentic self-expression.

Or consider Billy Porter – a Black gay man flaunting glittery gowns on red carpets with proud femininity. His Broadway talents took center stage while loud style choices shatter both racism and gender assumptions in the theater world.

Non-binary queer icon Jonny Sun inserts weird humor and vulnerability into social media, academia and the arts alike. Aromantic Jaiden Animation's quirky YouTube videos build community by shining light on overlooked orientations. Behind each trailblazer stand countless LGBTQ+ people uplifted in their footsteps.

The choice to live openly as one's true self above societal judgment redefines success. Yes, marginalization still exists even within progressive safe havens. Yes, basic needs and legal protections remain unmet for some in the LGBTQ+ community.

But the labels continually lose their limiting power when people shine through as their fullest selves. And society itself sheds conformity biases each time someone takes the stage unapologetically.

Reclaiming Queer Spaces

History reveals that LGBTQ+ people built vibrant cultures even under society's harshest spotlights.

Drag balls, open houses, working-class gay bars, lesbian separatist communes, friendship circles – these hidden havens nurtured family, faith and fulfillment denied by the outside world. Coded styles of dress, language, and symbols passed insider knowledge. Chosen families became survival networks where members could earn "legendary" status by overcoming hardship.

Reclaimed nightlife venues and districts like Harlem's drag ball scene or the early Castro district electrified with activism and self-expression. Magazines, books, zines and more recently internet sites archived once suppressed queer knowledge. Cultural cornerstones like voguing, camp style and ball culture seeped out from LGBTQ+ spaces to expand society's sense of diversity.

But mainstream visibility came at costs, especially to trans folks and queer people of color who built foundational spaces that lifted up white cis gender gay rights. Hate and gentrification battered these havens, even as their legacy boosted wider acceptance.

Rebirth keeps reopening doors as LGBTQ+ people continually carve out new realms aligning values, building chosen families, and nurturing arts and activism. Success follows from investing in community growth matching one's own success.

Today's reclaimed spaces blend online and real-world connection, such as Indigenous Two Spirit art shows, disability queer meet-ups, asylum seeker support groups and more. Mainstream visibility, legal rights and societal assimilation may expand, but smaller pockets of belonging continue breaking ground.

So let's keep celebrating beautiful countercultures that nourish LGBTQ+ wellbeing. And when society's toxic pressures to conform arise, we can turn to the safe havens where labels hold little meaning compared to living authentically.

Personalized Definitions of Success

Mainstream yardsticks for success may not apply to those who color outside expected lines. So how can we cultivate more meaningful self-measures aligned with LGBTQ+ experiences? The process starts with examining core values.

First, reflect on what matters most in your life right now. Dig beneath surface goals like job titles, relationship status, or badges of honor that impress others. What feelings, growth areas, and human needs fill your days with purpose?

Now envision your values unfolding over decades. Will the benchmark for achievement stay the same from age 20 to 90? How might re-prioritizing self-expression, chosen family, rest, pleasure, or legacy reshape the picture?

Defining success requires checking in with your core values at multiple waypoints. Change sparks new insights over the long run.

Ask Yourself

- Which mainstream "measures of success" inspire you? Which feel irrelevant or even harmful?
- If societal expectations disappeared, what would the ingredients for a fulfilling life look like just for you?

- Who are your role models across or beyond the LGBTQ+ community who embody success by being uniquely themselves?

Prompts to Unpack Core Values

Here are some questions to unpack what success means to you:

Fulfillment

- Which activities recharge you and put you into a state of flow?
- How could you spend more time following inspiring creative passions?
- Do you prioritize service, collaboration or solitude?

Security

- What level of financial independence or stability fits your vision?
- Would you trade income for more purpose alignment or work-life balance?
- How do you define family and community support networks?

Growth

- What parts of your identity unfold over time vs remain steady?
- What lessons do setbacks and challenges teach?
- How do you embrace fluidity of sexuality, gender identity, expression?

Legacy

- What meaning do you want to pass on through your life?
- What change or progress most motivates you?
- How do you positively impact your community?

Crafting Your Optimal Life Vision

Now comes the fun part: envisioning your best life by your own measure. This vision serves as the backdrop for defining and achieving success.

Imagine every area of your life as a unique garden plot, each requiring certain nutrients and care to thrive. These domains may include:

- Creative Expression
- Relationships/Family
- Physical/Mental/Spiritual Health
- Home Environment
- Work/Education
- Financial Security
- Community/Networks
- Personal Growth

You may combine domains or add new ones matching what nurtures you best. Feel free to get specific by describing ideal scenarios in each realm that capture your personalized success.

Some reflection questions for building your vision:

Lifestyle Details

- What does your ideal average day or week look like? What nourishes you?
- Do you prefer routine or spontaneity? Quiet or excitement?
- What physical spaces and belongings feel most like home to you?

Core Relationships

- Who comprises your family and community? Blood relatives, chosen family, friends, collaborators, mentors, partners, pets?

- What intimacy boundaries and relationship formats fit you best?

Personal Expression

- What aesthetic, clothing style, creative outlets, self-care, and movement feed self-expression?
- How openly can you communicate identity and values in various contexts?

Growth & Learning

- What stimulation catalyzes growth? Travel, conferences, documentaries, books, mentorship opportunities?
- What core skills and knowledge expansions keep you progressing?

Passions & Pleasures

- What energizes you and puts you into a state of flow? Hobbies, sports, crafts, sensory joys?
- How could you incorporate more delight into each day?

Contributions

- How do you wish your life to impact causes and communities that matter to you?
- What legacy opportunity most aligns with your values?

This vision board captures your unique flower ready to bloom. Let it guide you in making choices that help you flourish by your own definition of success. Revisit it whenever external pressures dull your clarity. Then use it as inspiration to take small daily actions toward this self-defined vision of achievement.

Turning Vision into Reality

Manifesting your optimal personal vision requires translating high-level dreams into defined steps and milestones. Break intimidating goals into bite-sized increments with built-in flexibility.

Rather than tackling every garden plot at once, pick a primary area of focus aligned with your current life stage and bandwidth. Within that realm, detail specific indicators of progress on a timeline that feels motivating yet realistic.

Here are examples across life domains:

Relationships

- Initiate monthly chosen family dinner rotation
- Attend LGBTQ+ friendship meet-ups
- Establish weekend routine of quality time with partner

Expression

- Enroll in queer art class at community center
- Create daily journaling routine
- Join theater troupe

Health

- Establish 8 hours regular sleep routine
- Walk 30 minutes 5x weekly
- Schedule annual wellness exams

Career

- Discover 3 inspiring LGBTQ+ role models in field
- Volunteer with related nonprofits
- Apply for internal promotion

Knowledge

- Read memoir from distinct LGBTQ+ perspective
- Sign up for virtual Gender Studies course
- Attend local Trans Visibility march

Financial

- Consult with LGBTQ+-savvy financial planner
- Reduce unnecessary monthly subscriptions
- Open high-yield online savings account

What matters most is simply taking the first step, then building momentum. Checking small successes along the way fuels bigger accomplishments aligned with your values. When you create new norms based around personalized wellbeing rather than outside expectations, living authentically becomes the path to achievement.

Overcoming Obstacles

Challenges will inevitably arise – external setbacks, self-doubts, societal speed bumps. But remembering your vision can provide perspective when arbitrary mainstream measures lose significance.

Focus energy on controlling what is within your power rather than fixating on perceived "failures" by conventional benchmarks. Be especially gentle with yourself when harsh internal voices amplified since youth still echo outdated societal messaging. Recognizing and quieting these pressures helps break their control.

Also consider obstacles as teachers revealing areas for self-care, resource gathering and deeper soul searching about alignments. Sometimes clearing space through release rather than willful striving opens unexpected doors. And don't overlook simple daily practices – meditation, journaling, therapy, support groups, nature immersion – that provide anchors of peace to weather storms.

When harsh judgments, either internal or external, arise telling LGBTQ+ people they are somehow less than, recognize this as society's defect rather than your own. Receiving external validation may still feel satisfying, but avoid putting self-worth on conditional hold pending such approval.

Ultimately, what others think does not determine the worthiness of your personalized life vision unless you forfeit your own gauging authority. The path revealing itself – however unexpected – becomes the right path when you remain rooted in your authentic truth.

Redefining Currency of Success

If left unattended, we all risk falling into society's default model of evaluating life progress with status, wealth and materialism. But those fixated solely on surface level gains often sacrifice deeper fulfillment and purpose.

What elements constitute the currency that opens doors of opportunity matching your values? Consider both tangible and intangible forms:

Knowledge Capital

Seeking empowering education, mentors and diverse lived experiences – our own and others' – offer perhaps the most accessible wealth for enriching perspectives. This capital comes not through formal credentials alone, but through curiosity driving self-expansion.

Mainstream yardsticks for success may not apply to those who color outside expected lines. So how can we cultivate more meaningful self-measures aligned with LGBTQ+ experiences? The process starts with examining core values.

First, reflect on what matters most in your life right now. Dig beneath surface goals like job titles, relationship status, or badges of honor that impress others. What feelings, growth areas, and human needs fill your days with purpose?

Now envision your values unfolding over decades. Will the benchmark for achievement stay the same from age 20 to 90? How might re-prioritizing self-expression, chosen family, rest, pleasure, or legacy reshape the picture?

Defining success requires checking in with your core values at multiple waypoints. Change sparks new insights over the long run.

Ask Yourself

- Which mainstream "measures of success" inspire you? Which feel irrelevant or even harmful?
- If societal expectations disappeared, what would the ingredients for a fulfilling life look like just for you?
- Who are your role models across or beyond the LGBTQ+ community who embody success by being uniquely themselves?

Prompts to Unpack Core Values

Here are some questions to unpack what success means to you:

Fulfillment

- Which activities recharge you and put you into a state of flow?
- How could you spend more time following inspiring creative passions?

- Do you prioritize service, collaboration or solitude?

Security

- What level of financial independence or stability fits your vision?
- Would you trade income for more purpose alignment or work-life balance?
- How do you define family and community support networks?

Growth

- What parts of your identity unfold over time vs remain steady?
- What lessons do setbacks and challenges teach?
- How do you embrace fluidity of sexuality, gender identity, expression?

Legacy

- What meaning do you want to pass on through your life?
- What change or progress most motivates you?
- How do you positively impact your community?

Crafting Your Optimal Life Vision

Now comes the fun part: envisioning your best life by your own measure. This vision serves as the backdrop for defining and achieving success.

Imagine every area of your life as a unique garden plot, each requiring certain nutrients and care to thrive. These domains may include:

- Creative Expression
- Relationships/Family

- Physical/Mental/Spiritual Health
- Home Environment
- Work/Education
- Financial Security
- Community/Networks
- Personal Growth

You may combine domains or add new ones matching what nurtures you best. Feel free to get specific by describing ideal scenarios in each realm that capture your personalized success.

Some reflection questions for building your vision:

Lifestyle Details

- What does your ideal average day or week look like? What nourishes you?
- Do you prefer routine or spontaneity? Quiet or excitement?
- What physical spaces and belongings feel most like home to you?

Core Relationships

- Who comprises your family and community? Blood relatives, chosen family, friends, collaborators, mentors, partners, pets?
- What intimacy boundaries and relationship formats fit you best?

Personal Expression

- What aesthetic, clothing style, creative outlets, self-care, and movement feed self-expression?
- How openly can you communicate identity and values in various contexts?

Growth & Learning

- What stimulation catalyzes growth? Travel, conferences, documentaries, books, mentorship opportunities?
- What core skills and knowledge expansions keep you progressing?

Passions & Pleasures

- What energizes you and puts you into a state of flow? Hobbies, sports, crafts, sensory joys?
- How could you incorporate more delight into each day?

Contributions

- How do you wish your life to impact causes and communities that matter to you?
- What legacy opportunity most aligns with your values?

This vision board captures your unique flower ready to bloom. Let it guide you in making choices that help you flourish by your own definition of success. Revisit it whenever external pressures dull your clarity. Then use it as inspiration to take small daily actions toward this self-defined vision of achievement.

Turning Vision into Reality

Manifesting your optimal personal vision requires translating high-level dreams into defined steps and milestones. Break intimidating goals into bite-sized increments with built-in flexibility.

Rather than tackling every garden plot at once, pick a primary area of focus aligned with your current life stage and bandwidth. Within that realm, detail specific indicators of progress on a timeline that feels motivating yet realistic.

Here are examples across life domains:

Relationships

- Initiate monthly chosen family dinner rotation
- Attend LGBTQ+ friendship meet-ups
- Establish weekend routine of quality time with partner

Expression

- Enroll in queer art class at community center
- Create daily journaling routine
- Join theater troupe

Health

- Establish 8 hours regular sleep routine
- Walk 30 minutes 5x weekly
- Schedule annual wellness exams

Career

- Discover 3 inspiring LGBTQ+ role models in field
- Volunteer with related nonprofits
- Apply for internal promotion

Knowledge

- Read memoir from distinct LGBTQ+ perspective
- Sign up for virtual Gender Studies course

- Attend local Trans Visibility march

Financial

- Consult with LGBTQ+-savvy financial planner
- Reduce unnecessary monthly subscriptions
- Open high-yield online savings account

What matters most is simply taking the first step, then building momentum. Checking small successes along the way fuels bigger accomplishments aligned with your values. When you create new norms based around personalized wellbeing rather than outside expectations, living authentically becomes the path to achievement.

Overcoming Obstacles

Challenges will inevitably arise – external setbacks, self-doubts, societal speed bumps. But remembering your vision can provide perspective when arbitrary mainstream measures lose significance.

Focus energy on controlling what is within your power rather than fixating on perceived "failures" by conventional benchmarks. Be especially gentle with yourself when harsh internal voices amplified since youth still echo outdated societal messaging. Recognizing and quieting these pressures helps break their control.

Also consider obstacles as teachers revealing areas for self-care, resource gathering and deeper soul searching about alignments. Sometimes clearing space through release rather than willful striving opens unexpected doors. And don't overlook simple daily practices – meditation, journaling, therapy, support groups, nature immersion – that provide anchors of peace to weather storms.

When harsh judgments, either internal or external, arise telling

LGBTQ+ people they are somehow less than, recognize this as society's defect rather than your own. Receiving external validation may still feel satisfying, but avoid putting self-worth on conditional hold pending such approval.

Ultimately, what others think does not determine the worthiness of your personalized life vision unless you forfeit your own gauging authority. The path revealing itself – however unexpected – becomes the right path when you remain rooted in your authentic truth.

Redefining Currency of Success

If left unattended, we all risk falling into society's default model of evaluating life progress with status, wealth and materialism. But those fixated solely on surface level gains often sacrifice deeper fulfillment and purpose.

What elements constitute the currency that opens doors of opportunity matching your values? Consider both tangible and intangible forms:

Knowledge Capital

Seeking empowering education, mentors and diverse lived experiences – our own and others' – offer perhaps the most accessible wealth for enriching perspectives. This capital comes not through formal credentials alone, but through curiosity driving self-expansion.

Community Capital

Investing in personal relationships and social networks that share understanding, resources and emotional nurturing provides the supportive safety net we all need during difficult times. Mutual generosity of spirit multiplies personal capital.

Advocacy Capital

By speaking up for not only LGBTQ causes but also other progressive movements, we gain strength and allies for our community's upliftment. Shared struggles reveal our collective responsibility.

Resilience Capital

Having navigated narrow assumptions, LGBTQ+ folks build spiritual muscles to weather all kinds of storms. By remembering our ability to persist despite barriers, we claim confidence to reinvent horizons.

Time Capital

Taking back control of your schedule to align activities with cherished priorities ensures sufficient space for wellbeing. Protecting rest and play offers fuel for creative fire.

Legacy Capital

Wealth through accomplishments, investments and possessions gain deeper purpose when their use also serves to elevate your community both for current generations and those to come. Plant seeds for future blooming.

The world may limit how we spend mainstream currency passed down through generations. But we remain rich when we bankroll our lives with alternative capital directly accessible through living courageously, generously and consciously.

Check-Ins: Assessing the Journey

Remember, society's static labels can't capture LGBTQ+ experiences unfolding across a dynamic spectrum. So regularly checking in with yourself around growth and life progress allows fluid self-awareness to override external attempts at definition.

Do annual or even quarterly self-reviews around key dimensions of your vision board and personalized action plan. Celebrate embodiment milestones and course correct plans if needed.

To gain deeper insight, also seek 360 feedback from a trusted circle of intimates who know your authentic self. Ask what they observe as core strengths, areas of growth and signs of alignment with your best self. Consider keeping a journal capturing check-in reflections to spot patterns over time.

Review frequently to ground against draining messaging that no one can determine success except you – the author of your life. Claim sovereignty over your own gauges without waiting for outside stamps of approval. Then continue writing the story only you can tell.

Investing in personal relationships and social networks that share understanding, resources and emotional nurturing provides the supportive safety net we all need during difficult times. Mutual generosity of spirit multiplies personal capital.

Advocacy Capital

By speaking up for not only LGBTQ causes but also other progressive movements, we gain strength and allies for our community's upliftment. Shared struggles reveal our collective responsibility.

Resilience Capital

Having navigated narrow assumptions, LGBTQ+ folks build spiritual muscles to weather all kinds of storms. By remembering our ability to persist despite barriers, we claim confidence to reinvent horizons.

Time Capital

Taking back control of your schedule to align activities with cherished priorities ensures sufficient space for wellbeing. Protecting rest and play offers fuel for creative fire.

Legacy Capital

Wealth through accomplishments, investments and possessions gain deeper purpose when their use also serves to elevate your community both for current generations and those to come. Plant seeds for future blooming.

The world may limit how we spend mainstream currency passed down through generations. But we remain rich when we bankroll our lives with alternative capital directly accessible through living courageously, generously and consciously.

Success Stories Beyond Conventional Measures

While the letters in LGBTQ+ represent a community bound by shared experiences of discrimination, each person's life follows unique trajectories toward self-defined success.

When society's constraints loosen through increasing legal protections and societal acceptance, queer folks expand visions of fulfillment centered on authentic personal truths rather than conforming to mainstream validation.

Diverse success stories reveal that no one template dictates a life well lived. By uplifting queer joy and resilience across the spectrum, we widen notions of achievement rooted in courage, compassion and community.

Growth Unbound

After decades spent imprisoned by fear while building a family and career in dense fog, Wanda tapped into a glimmer of long-buried truth that her gender identity didn't fully align with living as a woman. Transitioning to live openly as a trans man in his 50s finally allowed breath and clarity.

Risking coming out meant weathering rejection by relatives and neighbors clinging to rigid assumptions. But peeling off suffocating layers to stand exposed in truth also drew new circles of support. Little by little, Walt rebuilt identity and community completely on his terms.

He savored little joys like hearing his new chosen name, dressing freely, and nodding silent kinship when passing other trans folks on the street. After retirement, Walt nurtured a new generation of LGBTQ+ youth finding their way, remembering the isolation of his own decades in hiding. He found success through boldly shedding denial so others might tread easier life trails.

The Alchemy of Art

Over years spent reckoning with the absence of Black and Brown stories in the ballet world, Michaela unleashed her multi-hyphenate talents to manifest the change she wished to see.

Writing, choreography and dance coaching fused to equip aspiring young dancers of color with proven tools to shatter barriers facing few leadership roles or complex storyline opportunities. Her programs nurtured technical skill and emotional resilience alike to meet systemic racism.

But Michaela's boldest success came through celebrating inclusive queer joy front and center on stages where LGBTQ+ lives historically got relegated to dramatic tragedy tropes or one-note stereotypes. Infusing dazzling technique with messages uplifting marginalized communities, her artistic leadership raised the barre for authentic representation.

Building Beloved Community

As the AIDS epidemic ravaged San Francisco's Castro district, Cleve Jonesmobilized his grief into ingenuity for the Names Project AIDS Quilt: Each hand-sewn panel lovingly memorialized friends lost with intimate personal details.

Stitching together tales of thousands, the ever-growing 54-ton tapestry drew global conscience, comfort and calls to action. Like fractals branching mathematical equations into infinite beautiful complexity, each unique life patchwork fit seamlessly into the larger breathtaking mosaic.

Today as threads increasingly memorialize a new generation, the Quilt remains a living symbol redefining timeless notions of legacy. Rather than individual fame, Cleve's vision elevated collective memory, mobilizing ongoing advocacy that rewrote laws and societal attitudes alike. By uniting community in healing action, his success endures through the lives honored and saved.

Leaving No One Behind

As a disabled trans Asian woman immigrant, Kayla resisted being boxed into single stories. Across overlapping marginalized identities, she discovered firsthand how societal bias compounds – making basic needs like healthcare, housing and justice inaccessible.

Rather than fight to prove human value at exclusion's intersections, Kayla invested in unconditional mutual aid networks embracing people without judgment. She led with generosity, assuming unseen burdens rather than asking people to justify receiving help.

Opening doors for those barely acknowledged built bridges across divides. Soon donations, care packages and volunteers streamed in – not out of pity or savior mentality, but shared respect.

Against towering inequity fortified over generations, Kayla succeeded through ground-up efforts simply recognizing one another's equal humanity. Not waiting for leaders, she led through radical compassion meeting individual real needs, celebrating every soul made visible.

The Legacy Ripples Out

Measuring achievement often focuses on tangible outcomes like awards, status and long resumes. But groundbreakers along the LGBTQ+ spectrum teach that influence echoes in small kindnesses long after earthly departure.

Take humble heroes like Marsha P. Johnson and Sylvia Rivera, working class street queens who marshalled New York's 1969 Stonewall riots birthing modern Pride. Unconcerned with credit, they kept pushing against criminalization to uplift marginalized communities through advocacy and care networks for trans youth and sex workers.

Or lesser known figures like Black bisexual blues singer Gladys Bentley, whose 1920s musical fame spotlighted fluidity generations before liberation. Bentley's courage to live openly with her partner and perform in signature tuxedos and top hat expanded narrow visions.

These trailblazers moved within complexity beyond easy labels. They drove progress not through seeking historical acclaim but by revealing truths once considered too dangerous or undesirable for mass visibility. The public stage simply gave space for unapologetic authenticity.

Their humble footprints mapping bolder trails reflect success through wallet-sized kindnesses, each a breadcrumb leading toward more inclusive futures. When we lift up unsung heroes expanding freedom for all, hope multiplies that each of us can seed transformation by simply living out loud.

So let us toast luminaries and local shamans alike who nurture community from the grassroots, neither grasping for credit nor stopping until justice rings for all. By celebrating diverse victories, we widen the circle to make enough room for every story and expand each soul. For within a spectrum of unlimited potential, no success needs be measured small.

Your Unique Spectrum of Success

When we challenge ourselves to expand visions of fruitful lives beyond society's narrow take, LGBTQ+ experiences shine light on blind spots. By embracing personalized definitions of success, we combat external voices trying to shrink or skew our truth. Your spectrum of success follows no formula but your own.

This final chapter recaps insights revealed across the journey:

Release Society's Shoulds

Remember the image we initially conjured of stereotypical "successful" personas before tossing aside pretense? Take time now to rediscover what latent assumptions and internalized messaging still unconsciously shape your self-judgment.

Does pride spring from breaking barriers or claiming hard-won terrain in spheres historically off-limits, yet steeped in patriarchal values of domination and exploitation? Do you diminish allies finding fulfillment through harmony, collaboration and nurturing over combativeness?

Keep questioning societal measures losing relevance under an LGBTQ+ lens. Support replacements that better nourish our whole communities and planet. Define legacy beyond accumulation and control.

Stand Tall in Your Truth

The exhale of living openly beyond suffocating closets builds courage muscles over time. But self-acceptance often remains an ongoing practice in the face external skepticism about everything from bullying and discrimination to who qualifies as family.

Remember that no one else occupies the vantage point of your distinct experience. So comparisons lose meaning, and credentials fade in light of embodied wisdom. Your sexuality, gender identity and expression follow unique rhythms only you can translate.

So tune out detractors lacking imagination to embrace diversity's fabric. Reject respectability politics judging your worthiness by conformity levels. Celebrate allies who uplift without centering themselves. And take quiet pride in your community's herstory revealing just how long LGBTQ+ brilliance thrived before societal acknowledgement.

Focus on the Controllables

Inequity undeniably still permeates laws, healthcare access, workplace discrimination, housing vulnerability and more across LGBTQ+ spaces. Safety itself remains uncertain, subject to political winds shifting protections and emboldening hate.

Acknowledging obstacles, even multiple compounding ones like racism and ableism intersecting queerness, rightfully fuels frustration and anxiety. But avoid projecting inner turmoil outward by policing others' expressions of joy, identity or ideological differences around shared goals.

Channel outrage over injustice into expanding resources and support for those made vulnerable by systems bigger than any individual. Recognize leaders across modest platforms enacting daily change. Find community aligning strengths and needs to build alternative safety nets, flows of abundance and vocations advancing justice.

Nurture Intersectionality

While shared identity builds bonds, stop short of demanding conformity around expression, politics or strategies. Philosophical divisions splinter solidarity, especially across generational lines. Collect strength from diversity spanning the LGBTQ+ spectrum itself.

Today's umbrella term centered on gender and sexual minorities risks overlooking how other marginalized identities compound struggles. Racism, xenophobia, ableism and classism all profoundly shape LGBTQ+ realities.

So nurture intersectionality. Amplify voices across the full spectrum, embracing the layered complexities united under Stonewall's symbolic riots led by working-class gender-nonconforming people of color. Build understanding of why no singular Gay Rights or Trans Rights lens captures all.

Lead with Compassion

When fatigue, resentment or hopelessness creeps in, recall the vision that first called you to care. Every small act of understanding chips away at ignorance upholding bias. Seemingly fruitless conversations plant seeds sprouting beyond view. Diverse representations slowly grow belonging.

And know that people learn best through experiential steps, not theoretical debate. So lead more with compassion than condemnation when worldviews clash around LGBTQ+ issues. Assume positive intentions while firmly confronting harmful impacts. Meet fear with empathy for its root insecurity.

Progress flows from patience, not force. The greatest legacies come through equipping successors. So never stop inviting people further along the journey toward embracing humanity's full spectrum.

Lift as You Climb

Pride means acknowledging the sacrifices of elders and activists alike who pushed open doors inch by inch in far less forgiving eras. Carry their torch not through superior militancy judging new generations' approaches but through uplifting those still vulnerable.

Rather than seeking seats at exclusive tables of power and wealth built on oppression, advocate systemic redesign. Mentor those following behind by revealing where uneven footing lies ahead. Craft access and CLAIM abundance for communities long marginalized.

Share stories, resources and platforms to elevate oppressed voices within the LGBTQ+ community itself. Make enough room for everyone to contribute gifts meeting their needs. Define leadership as empowering others to take the mic rather than forever centering yourself on stage. Know that sometimes lifting others provides the only truly safe ground to stand upon together.

Grow Your Garden

Remember your vision board capturing dreams in facets of life from purpose and relationships to self-expression, environments and more that nurture fulfillment just for you. Make choices aligned with those soul feeds, not arbitrary mainstream benchmarks.

Then take consistent actions, both symbolic and tangible, to cultivate growth in priority areas. What rituals, habits and spaces emblemize your authentic truth and values? Infuse daily life with practices and design elements reflecting inner truths. Make room for not only individual growth but also inspiring community.

When metrics for achievement center on personal alignment, contentment and generously uplifting others, you claiming authority over your definitions creates the success you wish to see reflected in the world.

Leading Your Own Parade

Take pride in how far LGBTQ+ people have come in just decades from shadows to center stage visibility – not seeking others' validation but loudly claiming self-love. With identity awakened, next expand belonging so no one stands solitary when the music stops.

Each small step to understand – historical context, the spectrum's scope, intersecting struggles – builds bridges further uniting marginalized experiences. By embracing the glorious messiness within LGBTQ+ spaces, the letters lose limiting power to define or divide.

While universal human needs exist across all people, honor too the peculiarity and contradiction within the queer experience itself. Hold space for each journey traveling at its own pace between coming out and more hidden milestones alike.

Rather than demanding conformity or completion, offer companionship allowing discovery. With support net surrounding, trust unfoldment even on uneven terrain. Progress flows not from perfection but persistence and community.

So let your pride reside not just in bold identity proclamations during designated festivities. Live it through everyday revolution upholding outcasts and outliers alike. For liberation's work remains unfinished until none suffer alone in isolation anymore.

The destination ahead exists only as the next bend along the winding road we build together. So dance to your own rhythm, let your freak flag fly high. Success sparks with each step along the lifelong parade route you blaze through simply being unapologetically you – living brightly across your own spectrum.

11

Conclusion

Release Your Inner Fabulousity

In the closing pages of "Radiant Rebels: A Comprehensive Guide to Queer Empowerment and Personal Growth," we find ourselves at the intersection of reflection and celebration. Throughout the journey, each chapter has been a compass, guiding readers through the vibrant landscape of the LGBTQ+ experience. From embracing the symbolism of the rainbow flag to fostering resilience, cultivating self-love, and redefining success, this book has sought to empower, uplift, and inspire.

The essence of "Radiant Rebels" lies in its invitation to readers to embark on a transformative journey, one that transcends the pages and intertwines with the unique narrative of their lives. The LGBTQ+ community, often marked by adversity, has shown remarkable strength, resilience, and an unwavering commitment to authenticity. This book stands as a testament to the beauty found in the diversity of identities, experiences, and expressions within this community.

At its core, this guide has been a celebration of individuality and an exploration of the myriad ways in which individuals can embrace their true selves. From challenging stereotypes to forging meaningful connections, dancing with abandon, and redefining success, each chapter has invited readers to engage actively in the process of self-discovery.

The journey of self-love, examined in Chapter 4, has been particularly poignant. It acknowledges the complexity of the LGBTQ+ experience, recognizing the internal struggles individuals may face as they navigate societal expectations and embrace their authentic identities. The chapter serves as a guiding light, offering practical tools for readers to embark on a path of self-acceptance and unconditional love.

Chapter 8, "Friendship Feathers," has emphasized the importance of chosen families and supportive networks. The stories shared within these pages underline the transformative power of meaningful connections. Queer friendships, often forming the backbone of emotional support, have been portrayed as vital components of personal growth and a source of strength in the face of adversity.

"Dance Like Nobody's Watching," explored in Chapter 9, invited readers to celebrate their bodies and identities through movement. Dance, presented as a liberating force, is showcased as a universal language that transcends boundaries and allows individuals to express themselves authentically. It encourages readers to connect with their bodies in a positive and affirming way.

The book concludes with Chapter 10, urging readers to go "Beyond Labels" and redefine success in a spectrum of colors. By challenging conventional notions and embracing individual definitions of success, the chapter encourages readers to honor their unique journeys. Success, as depicted in these pages, is not confined to external validations but is a deeply personal exploration of one's values, aspirations, and authenticity.

As we close the book, it's essential to recognize that "Radiant Rebels" is not merely a collection of words on pages. It is an invitation to join a movement of self-discovery, empowerment, and celebration. It is a call to embrace one's true self, challenge societal norms, and find strength in the diversity that characterizes the LGBTQ+ community.

May this guide serve as a companion on the ongoing journey of self-discovery, a source of inspiration during moments of doubt, and a reminder that each person's narrative is a vibrant thread in the rich tapestry of the LGBTQ+ experience. As we bid farewell to these pages, let the spirit of the Radiant Rebels live on in the hearts and minds of those who dared to explore, celebrate, and embrace the kaleidoscope of colors that make each individual's journey uniquely beautiful.

About the Author

Kian Sanchez is not your typical self-help author. With a pen that's as sharp as a comedian's wit and a knack for injecting humor into the most serious of subjects, Kian has carved out a unique niche in the world of non-fiction writing.

A self-proclaimed connoisseur of life's quirks and complexities, Kian's writing style is a blend of sassy charm and unapologetic edge. He believes that self-help doesn't have to be a snooze-fest of dry advice; it can be a rollercoaster of laughter and enlightenment.

When Kian isn't busy dissecting the mysteries of human behavior or offering snark-infused wisdom, you can find him exploring the hidden gems of the culinary world, sipping on espresso shots, or embarking on spontaneous adventures. His irreverent approach to life seeps into his work, making his books a delightful ride for readers seeking practical advice with a side of fun.

Also by Kian Sanchez

I F*CKING HATE PEOPLE: A GUIDE ON DEALING WITH DIFFICULT PEOPLE
Do you have trouble dealing with difficult people? Do you feel drained and stressed after interacting with them? Do you wish you had a way to communicate with them effectively and avoid conflict?

In this book, you will learn how to identify different types of difficult people, understand their motivations, and develop strategies for dealing with them effectively. You will also learn how to stay calm and collected in difficult situations, communicate your needs assertively, and resolve conflict peacefully.

Imagine being able to walk away from any interaction with a difficult person feeling confident and empowered. Imagine being able to build strong relationships with everyone you meet, even those who are challenging. This book can help you make that a reality.

Order your copy of How to Deal with Difficult People today and start learning the skills you need to thrive in any situation.